Fast Famous Women

75 essays of flash nonfiction

Edited by Gina Barreca

Fast Famous Women

Edited by
Gina Barreca

woodhall press

Woodhall Press | Norwalk, CT

Woodhall Press, Norwalk, CT 06855
WoodhallPress.com
Copyright © 2025 Gina Barreca

Cover design: Mary Lasley
Layout artist: L.J. Mucci

Library of Congress Cataloging-in-Publication Data available

ISBN 978-1-960456-27-4   (paper: alk paper)
ISBN 978-1-960456-28-1   (electronic)

First Edition
Distributed by Independent Publishers Group
(800) 888-4741

Printed in the United States of America

Contents

xi

Introduction

By Gina Barreca

I once opened for Joan Rivers. She was coming in from New York to do a fundraiser, and more than three thousand fans were at the Bushnell Center for Performing Arts in Hartford, Connecticut, waiting for her to begin. I was there to warm up the crowd—the academic version of a local garage band—and introduce her. As somebody who had spent her life working on women's comedy, Rivers was one of my idols. I could recite several of her older sets by heart: "The first time I see a jogger smiling, I'll consider it"; "I have a friend who's not good with her medications and confused her birth control pills with her Valium. She has nine kids, but she doesn't give a shit."

Eager as I was to meet Rivers and as devoted as I was to her work, I was entirely unprepared for how tiny she was. You could have put that woman in a Happy Meal. Yet she was larger than life—and women's lives, especially when Rivers first started working in stand-up comedy, needed to be let out a little.

And she was amazing: After listening to my short talk and introduction, she came up to me on stage and said, "I hate you. You're funnier than I am."

She said "I hate you" with such natural affection and authentic appreciation that it was like getting a big hug and a bouquet of roses. Joan Rivers announcing "I hate you" made me feel loved.

Why do famous women matter? We look toward famous women to see how they did it, and to map their pathways (learning what to do and what to avoid) in the process of discovering our own. Many of

1

the writers in this collection express their gratitude to the woman they've chosen as their focus—saying, in effect, "Without you, I could not have imagined becoming myself," knowing that without extraordinary human beings to do something first, or best, few of us would dare to do anything at all.

And as a woman, to become famous for something is to risk not only an eventual failure but to risk success as well. Success can be scary too, until you become accustomed to it. (After that, however, I hear success and fame can get all kinds of cozy.)

I loved gathering together *Fast Famous Women*, even though it's been the most complicated of the four books in the Fast Women series for Woodhall Press. Finding the perfect writers for each essay, working with the complexities of their individual choices, putting together the overarching conversation that takes place throughout the volume, and reveling in the sense of community the contributors created made this an exciting although daunting editorial project.

Even discussing the word "famous" was hard.

Does the nuance of the word "famous" change when applied to women?

Or let's ask the question this way: Is "famous" in fact the worst F-word you can call a woman?

Given that women have been advised for quite some time now that "The greatest glory of a woman is to be least talked about by men, whether they are praising you or criticizing you," fame would appear to be anathema. That warning about being too much discussed is from Thucydides' *History of the Peloponnesian War*, so it falls under the aegis of "quite some time." Ladies were never supposed to have their names appear in newspapers except for mentions of their marriages and their dates of death; even having one's birth mentioned wasn't entirely ladylike—and then discourteous people could always investigate one's age, which was also never mentioned. Nothing about women was meant to be mentioned. Women were like vases: silent decorative vessels always waiting to be filled, rather fragile, and placed where they might whimsically distract but never claim attention.

(Like vases, though, they could also be dangerous when broken, thrown, shattered, or used as a weapon, but such matters were rarely discussed—in public. It was often only after a woman decided that she did not care how she was judged, or when she realized she had nothing to lose, that she risked being a topic for scandal and weaponized her own femininity.)

It seemed natural, then, that men got fame while women got reputations. When a woman got a reputation, it was rarely a good one—at least that's how I remember it from high school.

What is the difference between fame, celebrity, infamy, and reputation?

Becoming famous and becoming infamous are positions earned: They arise from something that a person has done. Celebrity and reputation are, in contrast, things a person attracts, the way a navy-blue suit attracts lint. I asked the writers for this collection to choose a woman who captured their attention, inspired them, fascinated them, unnerved them, and remapped the territory they thought women inhabited or inherited.

The contributors themselves explain their own attraction to the public figure at the heart of their essays. I did not assign the roster, but instead invited the contributors to think of this volume as a table where they could invite any woman from any period in history to be their guest for a dinner party.

There are glorious women who do not make an appearance, but if nobody asked Joan of Arc, Cleopatra, or Dolly Parton to this festive event (although they would be wonderfully at home), we are confident they will be feted elsewhere.

And one of the most intriguing aspects of this collection is that not every woman at the center of an essay in this volume is a household name. My students no longer recognize the name "Lizzie Borden," for example, although girls who grew up when I did gleefully jumped rope to the grisly, girly recital of Borden's murderous acts. I learned about Mary Foy, the heroine-librarian (although many would consider that phrase redundant) from reading Nicole Catarino's essay; I learned about the dance-philosophy of "individuality within community" from Adrienne Lotson, who explains how Katherine Dunham became her "guidepost." I thought I knew Fanny Brice, but the conversation Caroline Leavitt imagines having with New York's iconic "Funny Girl" gave me new perspective on both of these great women. Molly Peacock and Phillis Levin talking about one another in one essay by both, writing as two brilliant poets who share an enduring friendship as well as esteem and acclaim in their field, offer both strength and nurturing by proxy. Hearing Eleanor of Aquitaine chastise us, her twenty-first-century counterparts, on our lack of progress is humbling and hilarious when presented by Kathy Krause and Tamara Caudill. And it is simply encouraging to hear Niamh Emerson confirm, when writing about Queen Maeve of Ireland: "Ancient mythological queens—they're just like us!"

Other writers reveal to us stories about boxers, Supreme Court justices, chefs, singers, aviators, union organizers, movie stars, poets, and pirates. Hearing about them, we laugh, gasp, nod, and sigh, and long to enter the conversation—and bring our own gifts to the action. We are heiresses; we have a legacy created by the famous women who came before us, one we must appreciate and one we must pass along.

Finally, because women who achieve public acclaim and fame are necessarily insubordinate, interesting, and unnerving, we know when reading this book and when talking about this book, we are in the very best of bad company.

Jane Lynch

By Jane Smiley

Dear Ms. Lynch,

We have never met, but I would like to make a proposal that I hope would appeal to you. I am looking for someone to act the part of me in a self-produced autobiographical film I am making for my children (and whatever suckers would actually pay to watch it). I am asking you because (a) you are almost as tall as I am, and (b) we have the same first name, and (c) you are physically adept (which I am not) and so would look more graceful than I do running around, riding horses, and punching various Republicans in the gut (which I have never done but have always wanted to). I do wonder if you would be comfortable wearing glasses all the time, and constantly taking them off and putting them back on and trying very hard not to lose them. The other thing that you might refuse to do is talk like someone from St. Louis: flat, sort of sharp, and occasionally squeaky. I know from watching movies and listening to Gabriel Byrne reading his books on audio that a lot of actors like to do accents, but maybe not that "Sant Looose" one. Anyway, you are adept at many things.

I would construct my movie around my four husbands and my children, so you would have to play me at 20, 29, 37, and 49. I have sent letters out to four actors, proposing that they play my husbands. The one who looks most like my first husband, when he was 22, is John Mayer, but he would have to wear stilts or those woodblocks that Humphrey Bogart used to wear when he was acting with Lauren Bacall. I'm not sure he would do that, but we'll see. Kit Harington looks a lot like my third husband, and I would go with Orlando

Bloom for husband number two. As for husband number four, we keep trying to run into Clint at our local Whole Foods, and we are also leaving letters around town, hoping that he will pick one up, but he hasn't so far. Maybe he would if you would agree to play me. He might also be willing to direct the film. The issue that I have with that is that I am going to write the screenplay, and I am sure he would want to change a lot of things. But I want this to be as true to life as possible. I wonder what you think about that.

Anyway, if I give each of the first three husbands half an hour on the screen, and then my current husband an hour, that's a two-and-a-half-hour movie. What do you think of that? My favorite movie of about that length is *Once Upon a Time in Hollywood*. As you may know, Brad Pitt recently moved into the neighborhood. If you want to come for a visit, you might set yourself up to have dinner with Brad Pitt at Seventh & Dolores. I think you would like a lot of the stuff there—very upscale. I like the charred octopus and my husband likes the maple leaf duck breast.

I know you have been in a lot of TV series and movies. About once a week we watch a couple episodes of *Two and a Half Men*, and I am always struck by your portrayal of Charlie Harper's psychoanalyst. You are kind to him, and insightful, but it is evident to the audience that you have your own opinions about whether he can change his ways. When I think of you as me, what I imagine is the same thing—eye-rolling, lip biting, a few private smiles as I do my best to put up with, well, not the ex-husbands, because all of them were fun and smart, but, you know, people at parties who follow you around and won't shut up. That sort of thing.

I discussed this idea with my two horses: Paras, a mare who is no longer rideable, unfortunately, and Frankie, whom I ride about three times a week. Paras has spent her life wanting to show off her beauty in a movie, and is very disappointed that no movie has been made of *Perestroika in Paris* (somehow, she had already booked her plane trip to France, in preparation for her "close-up," but we haven't yet signed any sort of contract and she had to cancel her flight). She is happy to play herself in my movie, and she will do whatever you ask of her as long as you bring along lots of sugar cubes. Frankie is more reserved, but he will allow you to ride him as long as you don't take him out of his comfort zone (which is rather small). The first day, when I asked him, he told me that he didn't understand what a movie is, but apparently Paras told him. How she knows I have no idea, but she told the animal communicator that in a previous life she was an actress, Virginia Mayo. She liked that life, but her experience revealed to her that humans live too long, and she went back to being a horse; even so, she still wants to be a movie star, and she said that when she was Virginia Mayo, she always envied the horses when she was filming *Fort Dobbs*.

Of course there is the issue of payment. Unfortunately, I am not a member of the 1 percent. My husband is going to film the movie with his iPhone, once he figures out how to use it (it is a new one—he had the previous one for ten years). I suggest that you take all the proceeds, whatever they are, of the film and keep whatever you want and hand out the rest to your fellow actors as you see fit.

If you would like to continue this discussion, we can meet somewhere. I understand you live in Montecito. I live in Carmel Valley, and Atascadero is exactly halfway between our place and yours.

8

Annie Oakley

By Betsy G. Kellem

Annie Oakley Comes Out Shooting

Annie Oakley could hit a bull's-eye every which way from Sunday. She could pop the ace off a playing card, shoot an apple off her dog's head, or turn her back to the target and hit it anyway, using only a small round mirror as a guide for the rifle resting over her shoulder.

The woman known as "Little Sure Shot" was an A-list celebrity during the late nineteenth and early twentieth centuries, renowned for her sharpshooting prowess over a seventeen-year run with Buffalo Bill's celebrated Wild West spectacular. But her most famous bull's-eye may have been the one she landed in 1903 against William Randolph Hearst and his newspaper empire.

In 1903, Oakley was at the peak of her career. She was a legendary Wild West performer, had been lauded by Queen Victoria, and had parlayed her fame into a starring role in the Broadway play *The Western Girl*, written just for her. With her beloved husband, Frank Butler, at her side (they met when teenaged Annie beat Frank in a shooting contest and told him she liked his dog very much), Oakley carefully managed a career that not only celebrated her skill but also held her up as a model of proper femininity. She had reason to be exacting. Born Phoebe Ann Moses in Ohio in 1860, the future Annie Oakley matured quickly as a matter of survival. Sent to work at age 10, she escaped abusive foster guardians (who she called "the Wolves") and returned to her widowed mother and siblings. She would support them by hunting small game with her father's gun. Lively, pretty, and able to shoot the flame from a candle, she was an eager competitor

9

and crowd favorite. She hewed to her mother's conservative Quaker morals, which meant no flashy costumes, makeup, or extravagance. From the chaos of her youth, Oakley enjoyed the simple, practical pleasures afforded by life on the road: steady employment with her husband, access to fine guns, and a collapsible bathtub that fit in the corner of her tent on the show lot. For generations of Americans nostalgic for the mythic West, Oakley was an icon of upright Western womanhood.

Her image was her dearest possession, and Oakley curated it carefully. She noted with pride that during years on the road, "a crowned queen was never treated with more reverence than was I by those whole-souled western boys." She was therefore appalled when, on August 11, 1903, an article ran in papers across America alleging that Annie Oakley had been arrested on cocaine charges. Readers learned that beauty and prestige had left the "most famous woman rifle shot in the world," who slumped tearful and destitute in a Chicago jail cell. Coverage claimed she had stolen a man's pants to support "an uncontrollable appetite for drugs."

Nothing in the article was true, and the woman identified as Oakley was in fact an impostor. This was not unheard of in the age of "yellow journalism"—newspapers of the era, particularly those owned by magnates Joseph Pulitzer and William Randolph Hearst, regularly printed pulpy, sensationalistic stories that put sales before accuracy.

Oakley was incensed. Though newspapers soon issued errata confirming that the sharpshooter "is not a cocaine fiend and she is not a police charge in Chicago," burying corrections in small print did not convince Oakley that her image had been restored. To clear her name, Annie Oakley filed fifty-five separate libel cases against the newspapers that had maligned her. Between 1904 and 1910 she put her shooting career on hold and crisscrossed the country to hire lawyers and appear in courtrooms. In 1906 a frustrated Hearst tried to stop the onslaught by sending a private eye to Ohio to dig up dirt on Oakley. None could be found.

Annie Oakley won fifty-four out of fifty-five lawsuits (one loss, in Virginia, assumed that no one would have believed the article anyway). Folks assumed Oakley made a fortune from the suits, but court winnings were barely offset by travel and litigation expenses, plus lost income from missed shooting performances. But in the end, Oakley got what she wanted: control and vindication.

Even her opponents could not help but love Oakley for being as deadly in court as she was with a gun; a paper in Hoboken, New Jersey, sent her a letter that read:

Dear Mrs. Butler:
Although you dug into us for three thousand 'Iron Men' at a time when three thousand was a large sum with us—you see we still love you.
Yours very truly,
The Hudson Observer

Fanny Brice

by Caroline Leavitt

Already, I'm thinking this is a mistake. First, I'm a vegan and the Stage Deli is Carnivore on Skates. Second, I have loved Fanny Brice forever, but loving is different than knowing, and what do we have in common? I don't sing. I don't dance. We live in different times and we're totally different women, aren't we? But Fanny Brice is here and to get to her, I have to maneuver around all the flashing lights of the media, notebook in hand. They're here for her, not me, and I feel that old insecurity burrowing into me, that shyness I've worked so hard to conquer. Will I be enough? Will she like me?

Fanny's already in the back, and I can't help but stare. I've seen Barbra Streisand and Michele Lee inhabit her. But here she is, the real deal, and suddenly everyone else portraying her seems synthetic to me. I'm trying to inhabit a persona myself, the novelist who is at ease with a famous person. Ha-ha. Good luck. "You're so real," I say.

"Everyone thinks they know me," she says. "But no one ever really knows us unless we let them, right?" She winks. "Anyway, put the notebook down. We'll talk like people here."

Fanny orders the hot pastrami. I, a vegan, order a baked potato. Fanny studies me. "I get feelings about people," she says. "If you lived in my time, we'd have been friends, making mischief together." She raises one brow comically, and I can't help it; I laugh, my shyness evaporating.

While we eat, she tells me about Nicky Arnstein; but while I see him as Omar Sharif, in real life, she tells me, he looked like someone scrambled his features like eggs. He wasn't a suave gambler but a petty crook who was in prison twice. She paid his legal fees. "He looked bovine, but I was the cash cow," she says. "I didn't care what anyone said. I loved the lug."

She makes me want to open up, to be myself. I tell her I've loved my share of bad men, and she perks up. My first husband booted me out of our house, and I didn't know why until the longtime lover I never knew he had introduced herself to me. I lived for two years with a writer who didn't want me to eat, who thought my ninety-five pounds was too hefty. I was only able to leave him when he went into my computer and put in other words to "make it funnier."

"Never let anyone change who you are," Fanny says; then she reaches across and takes my hand and I feel a shock of warmth. "I left Nicky, but I was desperate for him to stay. But you left your rotter for good." She pats my hand and then lets it go. "I could have learned from you. You did good," she tells me, and I sit up straighter, because, yes, I did.

Fanny primps at her hair and takes out a bright red lipstick and slashes it across her mouth. She offers it to me, and I politely shake my head. Too bold for me. And then I ask her, and I hesitate here … if she thinks that women who are … unusual looking … have to be funny to be liked. I'm embarrassed that I asked such a question, but I think about my terrible years growing up; how I was mocked because I was smart and different, because my clothes were in as much chaos as my hair.

"Oh, honey, we're gor-geous," she says, and it's clear she believes it. It radiates off her. "And I'm funny for me—not for any guy. Hey, personality is beauty, not looks."

That's when I make a decision. "I'll take that lipstick now," I tell her, and she laughs and gives it to me, and then I have a red glamourous mouth, too.

"Never hold back," she tells me. "You gotta always be fearless. Don't hurt people, but don't care about what they think, either. As Sondheim says, don't worry so much about being nice, which is different than being good."

It tickles me that she knows Sondheim, but she's bringing out the bold in me; I feel so buoyed in her company, I'm wondering why I ever was anxious about meeting her—about meeting anyone. I can see the flash of the cameras coming closer, but I no longer feel nervous.

"Hey, I've got an idea," I say. "Let's sneak out the back, away from this glare of people thinking they know us."

"But you and me. We'll know." She jumps out of her seat.

Hey. I'd follow her anywhere—and now Fanny Brice is following me, out into the world, into the real.

Maya Angelou

By Leighann Lord

My Maya.

Well, it's disingenuous to claim Maya Angelou as mine, but don't we all kinda feel that way? She sat next to me once in First Class on an early-morning flight. I can't tell you where I was going or coming from, most likely a comedy gig. I really don't know. All I remember with any clarity is that I was sitting next to Maya Angelou.

I had boarded early and was ensconced in the window seat, selfishly hoping the one next to me would remain open. I looked up and saw Her coming down the aisle. At first I thought, "Hmm ... she looks familiar." I think this was my brain's way of protecting me from taking in all at once the reality of who I was seeing.

Alice Walker? Cicely Tyson? And then ... "It's Her. It's Maya Angelou!"

I stared—well, I tried not to and failed—as She walked up, stopped at the empty seat next to me, and began sitting down. I'm not schizo-phrenic, but the voices in my head became a screaming mob:

Stop staring.

I'm not staring.

Yes, you are.

Okay, I'm staring.

Well stop it. You're being creepy.

Am not.

Are too

Are you gonna say something?

What? No. It's Maya Angelou!

Exactly! It's Maya Angelou! You can't be rude.

But maybe She wants to be left alone.

Just say "Hi." Don't try to sit in Her lap.

Fine.

Fine.

Okay.

Okay.

Well, hurry up and say something before it gets weird.

I took a deep breath to get my heart out of my throat and said, "Good morning."

She said, "Good morning."

And that simple exchange of pleasantries was all I could handle. That's right. I get paid to essentially talk for a living and now I couldn't. I had no words, at least none on the outside. On the inside it was the Tower of Babel:

Oh. My. God.

She spoke to me. Did you hear that? She spoke to me!

See, that wasn't so bad.

I know.

Should I say something else?

Oh, for the love of God, no.

Why not?

Because you'll embarrass us!

And so I sat there quietly reading my book. And by reading I mean staring at type on a page. Don't ask me what the book was. I have no idea. All I remember is that I was sitting next to Maya Freaking Angelou. How I wish I had been reading *And Still I Rise* so the voices in my head could've debated about asking for Her autograph.

A flight attendant asked Ms. Angelou if She wanted anything to drink. Without missing a beat She said, "I'll have a vodka and orange juice."

The voices in my head said, *Well, damn. Is that why the caged bird sings?*

And it wasn't even ten a.m.

As the flight got underway, the Phenomenal Woman took out Her laptop and the voices said, *OMG, Maya Angelou has a laptop?*

Of course She had a laptop. But somehow I thought She crafted Her brilliance with a feather quill and parchment. And then I thought:

Maya Angelou is gonna write a poem right here, right now, while She's next to me! Is this really happening?

This is happening!

I had to see what She was writing. I just had to. You understand that don't you? And so, as nonchalantly as I could (which means not at all) I shifted my position in my seat so I could see Her computer screen from the corner of my left eye. And that's when I saw that Maya Angelou was playing solitaire.

You heard me. Solitaire.

And just like that she was transformed into a real person, a human being: My Maya. True, the vodka and orange juice before noon should've clued me in, but I'm a slow learner. I eased back into a comfortable position in my seat, and the voices were quiet for the rest of the trip.

And now that My Maya has taken her final flight, her seat next to me, while vacant, will never be empty.

Good night, My Maya. We'll miss you. Safe travels.

Salma Hayek

By Luisana Duarte Armendáriz

"*¿Rojos o verdes?*"

Nothing beats spicy chilaquiles for breakfast as a cure for being hungover. The tanginess of the tomatillo cuts through the nausea, and the heat wakes you up. Fried tortilla chips help soak up all the alcohol. As I watch Salma Hayek pour the steaming green salsa over the chips then add shredded cheese, a fried egg, and a side of refried beans, I raise a silent "Thank you" to God that we are both Mexican.

"What a night," she says, holding her *café de olla* with both hands as she sits next to me.

I still cannot believe she pulled it off. Walking in with a whole mariachi band to the celebration of the Cannes Film Festival's seventieth anniversary. Imagine this opening line of a joke: A mariachi band walks into the Cannes Film Festival ...

If anything had gone wrong, she could have been the punchline of that joke. Instead, Salma, the ultimate rebel, embraced her roots and made them her strength.

"Stereotypes are gained. There is no better stereotype to embrace and put into practice than the party-loving, mariachi-singing, tequila-drinking Mexican. We work hard, so we must also party hard to balance things out."

"So, how do you do it?" I ask, letting my last forkful of chilaquiles hover a few inches from the plate. I know the conversation won't end when I finish eating. There's always the *sobremesa*—that liminal space after a meal when you are done eating but no one gets up yet. No one rushes to bring the check over. No one heads out to their next activity. You just sit and enjoy each other's company after a meal together.

"You have to wait for the 'quick to judge people' to leave the party," she says. "I knew the boring people would leave early. Boring people always leave early. Then the Mexican in everyone comes out to play."

And as we discovered, everyone who stayed had a little bit of Mexican in them. You just have to coax it out of people. Mariachi is an excellent way to do it.

"And look at what the boring people missed," she adds.

It was a thing of beauty. Seeing actors, directors, famous people from all over the world cram around the "Mexican" table. Wanting to be invited into being Mexican. Because there's something about mariachi that does that to people. The goose bumps that you get listening to the first notes of "*Son de la negra*" or when singing the last lines of "*Mexico lindo y querido*," begging to be brought back to Mexico after death. We couldn't bear being interred away from our land.

The Cannes attendees did not need to beg to be included. We are an extroverted and welcoming people. It has been intrinsic to our culture since its inception. It happened with the *Conquista*. We, the mestizo people, are a product of this. From Ashkenazi Jews being chased out of Spain, to the Lebanese refugees fleeing the Ottoman empire or the Six-Day War, even Chinese immigrants settling in Mexico after working in the United States. And that's during the hard times. Just imagine what we can do during the good times.

It was a genius move on Salma's part. Bringing a piece of home (via Paris, because there are no good mariachi bands in Cannes) to sing songs to celebrate, to mourn, to court. But that is exactly what you must do when you live far away from the country that raised you. You need to tether yourself somehow.

The breakfast *sobremesa* continues. Cups of coffee are drained and replenished.

"Do you think you'll ever go back home?" I ask, wondering if returning home is in my own future.

"I don't know. I miss it. Of course I miss it. My Mexican-ness is ingrained in every cell of my being. But guess what? If I'm going to bring it to wherever I am, I better create an outlet for it. And that's why all my kitchens have to be Mexican."

There's wisdom in that. The center of the home is always the kitchen. There is so much in us that revolves around food and the kitchen. Making the center of the home a natural extension of the center of one's identity makes total sense.

"Weren't you afraid they would kick you out and never invite you back?"

She looks at me, thinking. Takes a sip of coffee and smiles.

I wonder if this *sobremesa* with my *paisana* Salma will extend to lunch. It has happened before.

Phillis Levin
& Molly Peacock

By Molly Peacock and Phillis Levin

We eat while we talk about our poems, effusing over every dish because, well, the artistic life is all about taste. We are close friends who don't think that role models need be distant idols. For almost half a century, while modeling for each another distinct ways to make the art we love, we've been eating everything from fried zucchini flowers to Stilton cheese. Just to introduce you to our way of sharing and munching and modeling, we are the American poet Phillis Levin and the American Canadian poet Molly Peacock—and we've composed these paragraphs together. Molly drafted them and Phillis refined, suggesting some ideas and phrases and inserting a quote. You're hearing Molly's voice, yet you're also hearing Phillis's vocabulary and thoughts. For us, one plus one equals three.

We met in Baltimore, Maryland, in 1976, at the Johns Hopkins University Writing Seminars. Twenty-two-year-old Phillis would write all day and never think about getting herself a meal. Twenty-nine-year-old Molly had been married, then divorced, and she wrote most of the day, too—though by four o'clock, she was thinking about dinner. Molly had been preparing food for her family since the age of twelve.

Molly says: When I started cooking for us, I didn't realize Phillis hadn't ever been allowed to choose what she would eat as a child. I, on the other hand, would dream up what I wanted to eat, and my mother would buy the ingredients or, better yet, would secret us to a fave restaurant while my dad was passed out on the couch, sleeping the dead snooze of a man who'd wake up with a massive hangover. Her friend, a waitress at that restaurant, would deliver us a feast—on the house.

(But it wasn't until Phillis was eighteen years old in college that she was faced with options and had the freedom to select her food. For her entire freshman year in college, she ate alone, relishing her solitude, and not yet comfortable dining with other people...)

Phillis says: I ate alone because I so much enjoyed having choice and not being observed or judged. The dining hall at Sarah Lawrence College offered food as excellent as a restaurant. They even served roast suckling pig for Christmas! As a child I had learned not to want anything. So I seemed an ascetic. But I was really a total sensualist. When Molly and I met, I was very porous, whereas she had clear contours. She enjoyed wanting things and had no compunctions about saying so.

In October 1976 in Baltimore, when we were making the first steps in what would become two lifetimes writing poetry, we found ourselves in a restaurant booth enthusiastically ordering food. So began our forty-eight-year friendship in poetry—with meals in no-frills diners to brass-barred brasseries.

A beet salad or a lemon poppy-seed pancake enhances our arcane, secret sort of table-size refuge for the adults we are, and the children we were, and the (very different) poems we write—even though we are completely in sync as we look at a menu. Our eyes land on certain dishes we both instantly want to order. We divide just about everything in half and share. Sharing applies to reading too, for we rarely meet up without at least one new poem to muse over. As we eat, we talk, reentering our earliest capabilities to perceive. We love owning those feelings that were ours alone and could never be taken away from us by challenging or threatening adults. We feel utterly alive as we dive into layers of baked eggplant or savor single pomegranate seeds. Eating, that elemental act, brings up our earliest preverbal years, what we touched and smelled and saw, things that fueled our poetry before we even had language.

We are now seventy-six and sixty-nine, sitting in the kitchen of her stone cottage in Connecticut, where she has just made a superb omelet. Between us, we've written a baker's dozen books of poetry: Molly, seven; Phillis, six. When we began our friendship, we were continents apart aesthetically. We were worlds apart in origins and class. You couldn't tell we were friends by our hair. Phillis's is luxurious, Pre-Raphaelite, long, and brunette. Molly's? Straight, fair, and bobbed. In our decades together, other relationships have slipped and slid away. Sometimes, one of us has lived alone, without a primary love relationship; sometimes, the other has. We both have reveled in the deep pleasure of profoundly satisfying marriages, though Molly lives solo now, after her husband passed away.

Moo Shu pork, black bean sauce, steamed pea shoots. A frisée salad with chèvre? A baguette? How about a chicken salad sandwich on multigrain with a pickle? Phillis and Molly have never dieted together. We always choose full cream, full butter; we've never substituted low fat for anything—certainly not low-fat poetry. Microscopic, opinionated critiques, to us, are the low-fat response—trying to tell one another what to do. We never critique one another's poems. We show them to one another at the end of a meal—after a large-breasted, large-bellied grandmotherly waitress brings us chunky borscht, or a harried hipster trots out our cucumber sandwiches. "Oh, look what you did in this line!" we might say to one another. "That's interesting," Phillis will exclaim and then suddenly start quoting a philosopher she has read.

Phillis has a kind of thesaurus of alternative words in her mind and a lyrical instinct. Molly has a sense of sequence, a narrative instinct. But a dexterity with syntax is central to us both. Phillis has often prompted a discussion of a sharper word for something Molly is trying to say in a poem, but she would never insist on it. Molly has often begun a dialogue about how the circumstances of one of Phillis's poems unfolds, but this conversation is out of curiosity. It can provoke a discussion about how events unroll, or unravel, or concatenate. Together, we arrive at a dialectical entity—and possible solutions to each of our dilemmas. Synchronicity tempered by a respect for complexity is probably the recipe for how we've lasted—provided there's mystery too. But perhaps the basic reason is a matter of taste. Taste is discernment. It's not eating to get full. It's about pleasure, both the pleasure of poetry's mouth music and the kinesthetic bliss of food's texture. The progress of a meal. The growth of a poem.

How is it that our interchanges have remained so focused and pristine? Ritual. Like the ritual of a hotel afternoon tea itself. Our custom is ceremonial, comprised of a meal with a postscript of silently reading words on paper, then bursts of our responses and associations with gentle suggestions. Our exchange has an aura of sacrament along with an atmosphere of parallel play, plus an ambience of parental mirroring. Perhaps a quote from an address that British poet Charles Tomlinson gave in 1967, when Phillis was in eighth grade and Molly a junior in college, might illuminate: "The poem in itself is a ceremony of initiation.... It is a rite of passage through a terrain which, when we look back over it, has been flashed up into consciousness in a way we should scarcely have foreseen."

We are careful of each other. And we take care of each other—a little bit like the waitstaff who cautiously clear the plates as we peruse our papers (oh yes, we are committed to paper) and talk, quietly circling the intense concentration of our postprandial back-and-forth.

"How can I explain to people that we don't critique each other?" Molly asked Phillis after Phillis had read this part of what she'd drafted.

"Say it's like a studio visit," Phillis said. Yes, our many tables have been our studios. Actually, a table for two has the proportions of a piece of paper. Could it be that we are writing our meals? Does our sharing create an overlay, like a shadow-poem hovering over the poems we have both brought to the table? Is our partaking of each other's work akin to breaking bread? We're digesting ideas after all. We never have to fear a blank page because our page, our table, is set. It's like the terrain Tomlinson describes. The table is a mesa. There are the place mats (rectangular as stanzas) and our cutlery (utensils, like pens). And so we sit down, two sensualists, for whom one plus one equals three.

Eleanor of Aquitaine

By Tamara Caudill & Kathy Krause

Lights.

The studio audience goes wild.

An elderly woman dressed in medieval garb folds her hands across her lap. Across from her, perched on a long orange couch, a young television host frantically checks her notes. Her eyes widen, then breathlessly ...

"Oh my God, you're Eleanor of Aquitaine ..."

More applause.

A beat. A cheeky grin.

"That's Eleanor, Queen of England and Duchess of Aquitaine to you."

Laughter. The host is clearly confused.

"You're not at all what I pictured!"

"Perhaps you were expecting Katherine Hepburn in a wimple?" *More laughs.* "I get that a lot. Katherine Hepburn was an inspired casting choice, I must say. That God-awful, ridiculous wimple, not so much." *Looks kindly at the host.* "Oh dear. Don't mind me. I'm dead. Continue."

Next card. Checks notes.

"So ... you had two high-profile marriages in the twelfth century: first to Louis VII of France and second to Henry II of England."

Interrupts. "How quaint. I see we are still talking about women in the context of men. I had much higher hopes for the twenty-first century." *Turns to the audience.* "Honestly, how much longer can the patriarchy endure?"

Cheers and raucous applause.

The host returns to her script. "Of course, Queen Eleanor was powerful in her own right."

Sharply. "I was."

"Granddaughter of the famous troubadour, Guilhem IX. Wait, no. Oh God, I didn't mean to ..."

"Don't worry, *ma cocotte.*" *Waves her wrinkled hand.* "It is clear that you have had an inadequate education and are obviously flustered by your brush with one of the truly great women in history. What could you possibly have done to prepare for an interview with a woman who could very well be your thirty times great-grandmother? Did you read what they wrote about me? I can only imagine the salacious stories preserved in parchment for all posterity."

The host hesitates, clearly uncomfortable.

"Oh please, do share, *ma chère.* It's been a while since I've had a good laugh. Let's clear up these little lies for you once and for all."

"So, there is the question of your crusade escapade ..."

"Which one?"

A naughty gleam appears in the host's eye. "Was your first husband so bad in bed you wanted to hook up with the great sultan, Saladin? According to the Minstrel of Reims, you had one foot on the boat to leave when Louis snatched you back."

"Ha! I can't speak to the perversions apparently going on in Reims, but rest assured I only seduce grown men. At the time of the crusade, Saladin was but a child. And though God knows *cher Louis* was nothing to brag about in the sack, I wouldn't have left him for a prepubescent boy. I left him for a virile 19-year-old!"

"Some writers also accused you of sleeping with your uncle Raymond?"

Tsk. "Listen, if you're going to just go down the list of everyone those idiots said I slept with, we'll be here all day. According to them, my vagina saw more traffic than the Camino de Santiago!"

Audience erupts in laughter. Taken aback, the host nervously flips to her next card.

"Did you really dress in gold and ride onto the battlefield, scandalizing the Greeks? Niketas Choniates compared you to Penthesilea, Queen of the Amazons."

"Oh, was that supposed to be me?" *Bats eyelids innocently.* "What a lovely story! What a flattering comparison! Although saying we rode into battle is doing it up a bit brown, the other ladies and I did do our part."

A balding man, clearly the director, points to his watch from offstage. The host deliberately skips to the back of the deck.

"Here's a good one: Reports say you single-handedly introduced troubadour music to both northern France and England? That sounds like a wonderful achievement."

"Now, there's a *petit* grain of truth in there somewhere. I love music; and my grandfather was a great troubadour himself. But single-handedly? Such an exaggeration."

"I also see that the writer Andreas Capellanus says you presided over courts of love."

"More like presided over the courts of my second husband's lovers! André always was one to embellish. But unlike you lot, we didn't stare into the palms of our hands like idiots and argue with invisible strangers for entertainment. We debated each other, face-to-face. Those were the days!"

In the host's line of sight, the director makes a curt gesture to wrap up the segment.

Disappointed, the host leans in. "Before we have to go, and God, this is so incredible! Eleanor, did you know you were the very first person I wanted to meet when I died?"

Eleanor reaches over to touch her hand, her gaze softening. "But my dear, why else are we here?"

Cut to black.

Lizzie Borden from the Grave

By Linda Button

Lizzie Borden took an axe.
Gave her mother forty whacks.
When she saw what she had done,
She gave her father forty-one.

I see you, you snot-nosed ratbags, judging me decades beyond 1892. You're no better than those churchgoing hypocrites of Fall River. Allow me to set the record straight.

First, call me Lizbeth.

Second? Let's discuss that horrid ditty.

Forty whacks? Forty-one? Try ten, you pinheads. Or nineteen, depending on whose skull was bludgeoned. But a children's chant has condemned me through eternity. Mother. Father. Axe. Whacks. Ha-ha.

Did you know I was acquitted? Twelve men found me innocent, after deliberating for barely an hour. They looked upon me—an upper-class lady, composed on the stand—and decided a mere woman couldn't commit such grisly acts. But what rhymes with "not guilty?" Nothing you idiots could devise, apparently.

I was a woman trapped in the amber of my time, a prisoner of place and circumstance. You modern women with your freedoms and independence: Imagine me, 32, the prime of life, forced to live with my 41-year-old sister, Emma, my father, and that mean old good-for-nothing two-ton stepmother, all squeezed into our tiny house near the harbor, among riffraff and immigrants.

I had brains. Social standing. I held positions of leadership within church circles: secretary, treasurer. In your days I could have worked and lived with indoor plumbing, which Father refused to install, despite his wealth. I served as my own chamber maid, hauling my "night soil" to the basement. Humiliating.

My allowance for dresses was so paltry—if some trinket caught my eye, shouldn't I avail myself? And the theft in Father and *Mean Old Thing's* bedroom. Perhaps it was I. So what? I had suffered decades under Father's meager thumb. He owed me. When he bolted his bedroom door after that, we had quite the locked-up little house!

Still, I was my father's daughter. The only ring he wore was one I gave him, not even a wedding band from his wife. Father taught me important lessons: money above all. Go for what you want, and never mind what others think. Know how to wield household tools, clean up after yourself, and never admit to wrongdoing. He gifted me the sealskin cape, my treasure. When I lugged it to Smith's drugstore to buy prussic acid, I meant to kill moths. The druggist claimed it was a well-known poison for humans! Who knew?

My days leading up to the killings? As if someone had put me in a vice and twisted. The squabbles and cold silences; Father hacking the heads off my beloved pigeons in the barn; the blasted heat of August. Today you bask in cool homes and refrigeration; we sweltered and ate congealed mutton stew off the stove for a week. The household suffered the "summer complaint." Father and *Miss Thing* retched in their room. The housemaid vomited out back. I ate cookies instead.

Then came the day that changed my prospects.

If you've seen the photos, you know why. Upstairs, behind the bed, *Mean Old Thing*—a mountain of flesh—slumped into a pool of blood, her piggy head quite shattered. That poor carpet would need scrubbing! Downstairs, dear Father reclined on the settee, as if napping. He almost looked content, save one half of his face chopped away. Shocking.

I called out to my neighbor, "Do come over. Someone has killed Father."

Investigations ensued. The police said only two people were in the house during the carnage: the housemaid and me. Surely, some man broke through all the locks. Amazing they never saw an axe-wielding lunatic run down the busy city streets.

Proof of my brilliance? No blood was found except for a bucket of rags in the basement, which I told police were from my "monthly fleas." The men were prevented by decorum from asking further about my menses. That dress I burned in the oven days later? Covered with paint! And what providence that my stepmother died first so that all of Father's riches flowed to Emma and me, not *Mean Old Thing*'s family.

After my acquittal, I bought a splendid home on the hill, christened my chateau Maplecroft, and lived the remainder of my days with dogs and servants. The church kicked me out and society shunned me. Me, pronounced innocent! Two-faced traitors.

You lucky women today, you have agency, you can earn money. I had to make my own fortune. I had to make plans and then execute them.

Joyce Chen
(Liao Chia-Ai 廖家艾)

By Darien Hsu Gee

Eggrolls and Bake Sales

In America you have to reinvent yourself. This is not your land, but the land you came to in 1949 aboard the SS *President Cleveland*, one of the last boats to leave Shanghai before the port closed and the Communists took over. You are thirty-one. There is hope for a future here. You settle with your husband and two children in Cambridge, Massachusetts. You have another child in 1952. You very much want to make America work. Your children attend the Buckingham School, and in 1957 you make two dozen egg rolls for a bake sale at the school bazaar. Within minutes they are sold out. That night, they ask you to please make more. You know enough to know this may be something.

All You Can Eat

A year after that bake sale, you open your first restaurant on 617 Concord Avenue—the Joyce Chen Restaurant. It is May 1958. This will be the first of four dining establishments, and many famous people will dine here: Henry Kissinger, John Kenneth Galbraith, James Beard, Edward Klein, Danny Kaye, Nathan Pusey, Paul Dudley White, Beverly Sills, and of course Julia Child with husband, Paul. Chinese students will flock from MIT and Harvard, homesick and lonely. This is not a chop suey joint. You elevate Chinese cooking and train American tastebuds, but you know to take it slow. You value authenticity, but you want to make Chinese food accessible.

Onward
In 1966 you divorce the husband.

Julia & Joyce
The part everyone forgets. Everyone remembers you as restauranteur, entrepreneur, TV personality. Less is spoken of you as a working mother of three, a divorcée with 1960s America and McCarthyism in the rearview mirror. America with McCarthyism still in the rearview mirror. So many comparisons with your friend Julia—you share the same set at WGBH after all, the French decor swapped for "Oriental" motifs such as wind chimes, folding hand fans, a bamboo-like plant in the background. You both have Ruth Lockwood—producer, friend, cheerleader. But Julia also has Paul. She has no children, no restaurant. You, however, are a single mom, a woman of color, an immigrant. Your hands are full, to put it mildly.

Speak English
They say it's your accent that makes the show challenging. One year, twenty-six episodes, no corporate sponsor. You have a voice coach, but still. Sometimes you spell words so your audience understands what you are trying to say. *Fowl. F-O-W-L. Main. M-A-I-N.* English is not your first language; the words will never roll off your tongue, yet you know exactly what you are trying to say. The words "adapt," "adept," "adopt," "Americanize." Also "assimilate" and "accept." You understand the language of this country. It turns out to be your native tongue.

Joyce Chen Cookbook
This is where I first meet you, in the pages of a hardbound cloth cookbook I find on my mother's bookshelf. The dust jacket has a watercolor painting of Chinese vegetables on the front, a black-and-white photo of you on the back. I have seen my own mother in the *Denver Post* holding chopsticks over steaming platters of stir-fried

vegetables. My aunt had a Chinese restaurant, a cooking school, has authored multiple cookbooks. Both have master's degrees, but this was their celebrity. They wanted to make America work too.

Wokstar

Call it grit. Chutzpah. *Nǎli*. Call it US design patent 221397S. On August 10, 1971, your first and only patent for a "cooking utensil," the flat-bottom wok. This isn't the only big idea you'll have, nor is it the only "Eastern cookware for the Western kitchen" you'll introduce over the years. *See* terra-cotta clay pots, stainless steel cleavers, kitchen scissors, dumpling press. In 1984 your bottled sauces hit supermarket shelves.

Memory

It's 2014 and you have been gone for twenty years. It is not the ending I would have written for you—an accident, then an illness, possibly Alzheimer's. You deserve a glimpse of the future, to see the flagstones you laid down and who got to walk upon them. It is the advent of foodies and bloggers and cookbook authors and—*āiyā!*— influencers. But in September 2014, your birthday month, the US Postal Service issues a Celebrity Chef Forever series, and you are your own "Forever" stamp, along with Julia, James, Edna Lewis, and Felipe Rojas-Lombardi. You, forever. The same smile that welcomes everyone at the beginning of the show and then at the end invites them to join you at the table.

Alex Guarnaschelli

By Cheryl Della Pietra

It doesn't make any sense, but I find watching the show *Chopped* relaxing. Why, when I'm looking for a welcome distraction, do I gravitate to the Food Network to watch a group of harried chefs take four disparate ingredients (squid ink, broccoli rabe, bison steaks, and gummy bears!) and make them into a cohesive dish in thirty minutes or less? It's because I'm hoping Alex Guarnaschelli might be one of the judges.

The plate is set before her, the chef eyes her nervously; then Guarnaschelli tastes the food, and what follows is a pause so pregnant, it could bear triplets. Her deadpan stare gives nothing away, but it's not intended to intimidate.

She's thinking.

Then, while the other judges are busy offering some version of "delicious" or "not cohesive," Alex will declare: "In the wrestling match between sugar snap peas, radish, and scallion, team scallion for the win."

The way Alex Guarnaschelli talks about food is the same way poets talk about love, or the Inuit talk about snow. Her language is layered and rich, cerebral even, involving nuances, ideas, and feelings so complex that those who are judged by her are left to ponder their relationship to food in a new way.

Of a stuffed eggplant: "I think the way you introduced broccoli and oregano actually created a delineation between the spinach and the kale in the basket."

Of a subpar crostini: "This is the crack in the boat that can make the whole thing sink."

Of a too-thick appetizer: "It's like a mattress with a tomato sleeping on it."

But her focus is not just on the food.

She's a psychologist. "Why are you upset?" she queries one distraught chef. "I feel a lot of heart from you," she encourages another.

She's a competitor. On *Alex vs. America*, where three chefs try to take her down: "This is my office. I'm going to sit at my desk right now; and there are these three people that are trying to take my desk from me, and I don't like that."

She's a taskmaster. On overuse of an herb: "There's enough rosemary in here to make one of those little sachets to perfume a dresser drawer."

Ouch.

She can at times be a little brusque, but she is no Gordon Ramsay. She merely talks to chefs in a serious way, treats them like the artists they are. Food is their canvas, an insight into what makes them tick. Why did you add the truffle? Why the choice of bacon? She's not trying to change their mind, necessarily. She wants them to consider—deeply—their relationship to the food they are preparing. Why did you make this, and why did you make it for me?

But the real reason Chef Alex occupies space in my mind—why I will never change the channel when I see she's on—is because she, like me, is Italian. There is something familiar about the way she talks about food. It's a family obsession. It's a personal statement. It's a flex. It's love. It's life. Watching *Chopped* or *Alex vs. America* or *Supermarket Stakeout* or *Iron Chef* or *Ciao House* isn't just an exercise in zoning out on a Friday night. For me, it is the ultimate comfort and deeply personal.

The best part of any show she judges is when the deadpan stare breaks into a wide smile, when the Iron Chef deems a particular dish "addictive." It's something more than a mere compliment. It's a five-star review. It's earning an "A" from the hardest teacher. And that's a role she plays as well, because Chef Alex has lessons for all of us, in eating and in cooking and in life: Respect the food. Respect yourself. Take it all seriously, but take joy in it too. Stand by your choices. Stand by your dish.

Beverly Cleary

By Alison Umminger

When Beverly Cleary's most iconic character, Ramona Quimby, age eight, is asked to do a book report on *The Left-Behind Cat*, she deems the work "medium-boring" and sets about finding a way to make the report palatable for her 8-year-old audience. After a failed dramatic rendering of the report, complete with a chorus of "meows," she laments to her teacher that the book wasn't, after all, very good. And why should a child read or sell a book that isn't any good?

Beverly Cleary, who lived 104 years, and sold eighty-five million books in her lifetime, wrote books that were very, very good and never, under any circumstance, even slightly boring. She believed that children deserved books that were well written, funny, and mirrored their own lives. When my daughter was seven years old, my husband and I were able to linger at restaurants if one of us remembered to add another Ramona book to the Kindle library. As a parent and a writer, I'm fascinated by the books that stand the test of time. Ramona and her family, with their cosmetology-school haircuts and fingernails-in-the-middle-class anxieties, reminded me of my own upbringing; and Ralph S. Mouse, who rode his tiny motorcycle, still calls to my imagination. Ramona in particular spoke to my twenty-first-century progeny, even though Ramona does *not* have a cell phone or a YouTube channel, probably because she is so consistently curious about and exasperated by the world around her. Cleary maps childhood from the inside out; and her own deep sense that there's something *universal* in human experience defies our current obsession with self-isolating bubbles. Ramona's deep love of a new eraser or non-hand-me-down pair of pajamas makes her journey relatable in its specificity, even if the details are not the reader's own.

The ability to recall childhood with deep clarity, but little sentimentality, is the vein of literary gold that Cleary instinctively knew where and how to mine. Cleary vowed early on that she would never write to passing trends, and her books belie a deep trust of her own voice and experience. How else could an only child write so convincingly about siblings? One feels when one reads Cleary that childhood is a space not so much remembered as reentered. Cleary's degree in library science certainly helped her understand young people's literature, but she was also an innate and gifted observer of her own life and the lives of the children and adults around her, which allowed her to re-create those spaces with just the slightest added touch of adult wisdom.

Middle grades author is one of the few professions that can create rabid fans while still allowing for the relative anonymity of the writer. That's a short way of saying that when one reads Cleary, it's all about the books. Cleary herself led a life every bit as interesting and engaging as any of her characters. Her first volume of autobiography takes the reader from her childhood in Oregon, through the Depression and the poverty she and all those around her endured, to the bus ride that will take her to California and her adult life. As she departs her own girlhood, she closes *A Girl from Yamhill* with: "My father kissed me good-bye; my mother did not. I boarded and found a seat on the station side where I looked down on my parents standing together, seeming so sad and lonely." The loneliness of an only child with unhappy parents whose deepest desires were at odds with each other's seems to be a part of her own experience that Cleary gives her characters. Sometimes, she seems to say, it all works out even if nothing works out.

Ramona's parents love her and her sister, and they fight over undercooked pancakes rather than mention their own interminable workdays and unfulfilled dreams. Somehow, everyone muddles through. The genius is that Cleary never stops to moralize; characters in her fictional worlds are basically decent, rascally enough to be fun, and held to the constraints of their own social and economic realities. In *Ramona and Her Mother*, the closest one gets to a lesson is Ramona's mother reminding her daughter, "Grown-ups aren't perfect, especially when they're tired." Truer words have not been said. Cleary seems intuitively to know that what children need are not cautionary tales, or dystopian fables, or wild escapes into alternate realities, but a reminder that the world—as they experience it—is real, flawed, and loving. If life is not always totally good and fixable, at the very least, it remains manageable. The fact that love is not always perfect doesn't make it any less true.

The quote that closes this memoir continues, "As the bus pulled out of the station, I looked back, filled with sorrow, as if I were standing aside studying the three of us: my gentle, intelligent father who had surrendered his heritage to support us by long days confined in the basement of a bank; my often heroic mother with her lively mind and no outlet for her energies other than her only daughter; myself, happy, excited, frightened, and at the same time filled with guilt because I was leaving my parents behind." The gentle clarity with which Cleary holds her own past mirrors the frank and reflective qualities of her most famous characters. Her writing is brilliant, funny, and touching—and she makes it look so *easy*. Is it any wonder that we still love living in Ramona's World?

Alison Steele

By Grace McFadden

In the warm, dim glow of a studio somewhere in New York, The Nightbird's fingers flit over the station's record collection. She slides a fader down, sucks on a cigarette, and then leans into the mic to implore her audience to take a moment to reflect with her as she winnows away the dark minutes until dawn. Somewhere, years before now, Alison is murmuring into a mic, switching from one record into another. Thousands of New Yorkers, hustling strangers new to the city, new to the state, new to the country, are slipping under the influence of her sultry and mellifluous poetry; The Nightbird's ethereal tracks offer a temporary respite from the churn of daily life, a nocturnal island for the ground-down and lonely, which is gone as soon as it comes.

In college, I used to host a radio show. For the first few years, I did my show most often by myself, in safe harbor if I could manage it—the block of airtime at night during which the rules for DJs are relaxed. Alone in the studio, I would picture my ideal listener. This person was a late-night traveler of some kind—usually a truck driver, for whatever reason—whose radio dial slipped to my show by chance. I hoped whatever I said into the mic would capture their attention for a moment, just that, and leave the vagabonds shipwrecked on my show wondering about that odd late-night station.

Fingers sliding up the faders, sly eyes looking out at the moon over the city, maybe the The Nightbird had the same fantasy as me: pilgrims making their way to or through her coverage area for the first time. Maybe the audience she pictured was the hordes of young and hungry minds left to their own devices in New York City in the early '70s. Maybe she meant to speak to the early-20s crowd, ground down against the recent acquisition of a full-time job, the threads of life still tenuous, swirling questions about future and identity getting caught and torn in the teeth of everyday life.

Or maybe I'm just projecting, as this is how The Nightbird found me: young and lonely, in my third new city of the year, trying to figure out how a life ought to be lived. See, on a warming Tuesday night in May, I hosted my last radio show. Five days later I graduated. Then I moved from the only place I've ever known to a new city, and then another, and then another. In each new place, I found myself wandering unfamiliar streets, asking the big questions The Nightbird implored her audience to consider. In my headphones, Alison Steele told me that I'd fucked up today, and that tomorrow would be miserable too, but for tonight I could fly with the Nightbird, her bard-like cadence and loping, unwinding songs crisscrossing my consciousness.

While many stations have archives, radio is not meant to be permanent. Words come cheap and fast. Songs aren't kept—they unfold recursively into the air, dissipating as soon as they appear. In the purest form, radio does not exist past the exact time and place it begins, like a real conversation. This is part of why I liked hosting a show. You might reach hundreds or thousands of people, but when it's over, only the memory remains.

In new rented rooms I read Shakespeare; I wrote poetry; I listened to the radio. I did these things most often by myself. There are no witnesses to those hours spent reading *The Tempest*, or the time spent walking in circles around a baseball diamond. The archives easily available for The Nightbird are similarly slim. The seconds in her radio broadcast unspooled like the days in my postgrad life: slow, contemplative, defined by their own ephemerality. On one of the few shows listeners can still readily find, she quoted *Much Ado About Nothing*: "What we have we prize not to the worth/whiles we enjoy it, but being lacked and lost/ why then we find the value, then we find/the virtue."

After I graduated, a friend became the program director of my college station. Back in some tangles of wires and drives, they said, were the recordings of my old shows. Would I ever want to hear them? I thought about it for a bit, and then said no. Those shows existed then and there. This is here and now.

Martha Graham

By Karen Henry

K. Martha, thanks for agreeing to this interview. What did you think of Agnes de Mille's book about you?

M. I didn't read it. I don't enjoy reading reviews, articles, or books about myself or my work. Agnes is a dear friend—we like to gossip together, and she has always supported my work—even though she does something quite different. Her Degas studies were magnificent. Those should be revived. *Rodeo*—I enjoyed watching the girl; she had fire, but her spiky movements didn't touch my soul. As for *Oklahoma*, well, that's Broadway. I had my own brush with that kind of work when I performed with the Greenwich Village Follies long ago.

K. De Mille says she felt like your adoring younger sister, and she stood up for you and your work, over and over—with evocative descriptions of ballets, including *Night Journey*, *Cave of the Heart*, and *Appalachian Spring* of course. She was impressed by the depth and power of your movement and your passion. But she also recounted disturbing moments when you slapped your dancers—men and women. She said that once or twice a boy stalked out in a rage after you hit him, but then you ran after him and, in a little-girl voice, told him it was because you cared—you loved him so much.

M. I did have my rages—once, I don't remember why, I was angry. Staring at myself in the mirror, putting on makeup for a Denishawn performance, I threw a bottle of body cream and smashed it against the mirror, which shattered into a thousand pieces. I simply moved to another mirror, applied my makeup, and went onstage.

K. You needed that emotional chaos to create your dances?

M. Light and darkness, good and evil; they are the same powerful force—standing against annihilation. I portrayed women of power in the throes of passion, grief, guilt, desire: Jocasta on the verge of suicide after her incest is revealed to her; Clytemnestra, the murderess murdered by her son; Medea, tortured by jealousy—figures of immense energy thwarted by fate, by desire, by the fear of retribution. All the things I do are in every woman. Every woman is a Medea. Every woman is a Jocasta. In most of the ballets I have done, the woman has absolutely and completely triumphed.

K. You've said that women are more ruthless than men.

M. I know that in a woman, like a lioness, is the urge to kill if she cannot have what she wants.

K. You have a reputation for being serious, pretentious even. And yet I've heard that you enjoy parodies of your work.

M. Fanny Brice, a fabulous mimic, did a spoof of my dance "Revolt," in the Ziegfeld Follies. She copied my makeup, hair, costumes, facial expressions, all my severity. At the end, in her Yiddish accent, she cried "Rewolt!" I saw it four times—but I didn't have the courage to go backstage. Danny Kaye did a takeoff of me with his Graham Crackers—remember that number in *White Christmas*, "Choreography"? He mocked my spirals and contractions and then broke into tap dancing. Everything has its place, I suppose. The best parody of me was done by a brilliant female impersonator, Cyril Ritchard.

K. De Mille enjoyed your sense of humor—something most people don't suspect you have. But why have your dances captured our imagination?

M. I reveal what we say we don't want to see but what we can't tear our eyes from. Joseph Campbell told me that I enter the world of the unconscious, tapping into the atavistic memory where fairy tales and myths are rooted. I became fascinated by Jung, but I had already been dancing the shadow, the anima, the forces that drive us, if we are truly alive. Isamu Noguchi made sculptural miracles for my sets—together we brought haunting worlds into being. Who can forget the shining, vibrating, bronze wire dress I wore as Medea in *Cave of the Heart*, the terrible cage and chariot that carried me home to the sun?

K. You've reached such a pinnacle, dancing at the White House, schools all over teaching your technique, and a company performing your masterpieces. Have you expressed all that you meant to say?

M. There's no satisfaction for the artist—there's a blessed unrest that keeps us marching and makes us more alive than the others. I have no peace—just the infernal urge to move.

Radclyffe Hall

By Susan Cosette

Darling one, may I offer you a brandy? Let me fix one for you, and another for me.

Do sit, be comfortable, and let's get on with it.

Well then, how *does* one speak of a long-dead queer person who self-describes as a "man trapped in a woman's body?"

My tale may seem commonplace to you, but please be assured that in 1928, I was *far* from customary. If there were others like me, they were most likely hidden away with maiden aunts in the Cotswolds, shivering in damp rooms.

I was called a "congenital invert." This was the nomenclature propagated by the likes of a bearded old eugenist turned sexologist, Havelock Ellis, who spewed his lies during my youth. If he had the chance to meet me, he likely would have had me sterilized. Not that I planned to have children in any event.

But darling, in your world now, I would simply be known as a member of what you call the LGBTQ+ community. That's not at all alarming to your generation, is it?

Have another brandy. Oh, would you care for a cigar?

Darling, few have heard of me, let alone read my poems and novels.

I am Radclyffe Hall, but I insist you call me John. My birth name, Marguerite Antonia, sticks to my palate like nasty Marmite spread on a stale, salty Duchy biscuit.

Unsavory, unwanted, unwelcome.

Marguerite was a petulant pinafored child raised in a drafty nursery schoolroom. Her hands large and clumsy, she had no desire to thread needles for cross-stitch. Her long braids were unruly. She did not wish to play mother to the cipher-faced baby dolls provided to her by absent parents. When Nanny was not looking, Marguerite flung the fragile porcelain beings into her fireplace. The sound of them crackling, then erupting into shards, was exhilarating.

Bad Marguerite.

Father left, and Mother took up with a singing professor, a sharp-nosed mustachioed man called Albert. They quarreled incessantly, and I despised them both. Suffice to say, there was little harmony at home.

Father left a sizable inheritance, and once I came of age, I was free to live as I wished. There was no need to marry, or to work. Off went the heavy gray bombazine skirts; out came the plus fours and sturdy tweed blazers. I regarded my curious new world through one eye, squinting into a monocle strung on a shiny brass chain.

Suddenly, everything was magnified—and magnificent.

I studied everything and chronicled all: the scowls at the market, the whispers behind slender leather-gloved hands, the cold emptiness that enveloped me each night before sleep. Surely there must be others like me, those whose voices and desires differed, but somehow were not wrong, unnatural, or immoral.

I amassed every experience and produced five books of poetry in nine years. I did, however, lose every woman I loved to men and marriage.

Then came Mabel.

In her 50s and twice my age, Mabel found me in Frankfurt. I was floating face up in the warm mineral springs, dark eyes fixed on an indifferent sky, praying decades of rosaries on my rough fingers as I was trained to. It was my comfort, my solace.

That evening at the casino, Mabel sat beside me and placed her chips alongside mine at the roulette table on number 27, my age at the time. The wheel spun round and round, finally slowing to its final *tick, tick, tick*. She squeezed my hand, and the croupier called our number.

"Ladies and gentlemen, we have two winners!" We took the money and went to my suite with a bottle of excellent cognac.

Sweet, fleshy Mabel. Pale, smelling of verbena and clove cigarettes. My lover, my true mother, more so than the stiff American woman who reluctantly gave birth to me.

Mabel baptized me in the claw-foot porcelain tub. I curled against her in the warm water as she washed my long hair. She toweled it dry, gently combed through the knots, and then carved it into an Eton crop, discarding the remnants of my past self into yesterday's newspaper. Together, we tossed it down the furnace chute.

My dearest, you are now John.

John produced novel after novel, one an international bestseller banned on several continents for immorality and obscenity because I dared speak my truth! To be thrust into the public eye after years of relative anonymity was unnerving. Derided, ridiculed, I became a spectacle of what a woman is *not* to be. But this was a temporary irritation, like the time I discarded stiff-heeled shoes and broke in that first lovely pair of soft leather walking boots to explore the misty moors.

Oh, my new friend, here is a leather-bound first edition of my best-known book, *The Well of Loneliness*. Allow me to inscribe it for you. One day my work will be studied at university, rather than being passed about in secrecy and shrouded in shadows.

Go now, and share with your silent sisters.

Sally Ride

By Anne Bagamery

Sally Ride: The Reluctant Role Model

My first professional ambition was to be an astronomer.

It was the early 1970s, and I was in junior high at a girls' school. Good at math, interested by the stars, slightly in love with my science teacher (hey—we all were), I wanted to see how high I could go.

That all crashed to Earth a few years later, when I encountered a girl-hating pre-calculus teacher in high school who, every single day, made fun of me and the other girls in the class for asking questions, giving the right answers, and basically just existing.

We were already socially unpopular because we were smart; now we were the butt of a teacher's ridicule, and it was OK for the boys to laugh at us.

I've done fine in life, but I've never stopped wondering what might have been if I hadn't been so easily discouraged from a career in science—or so hung up on what men thought of me.

That is why Sally Ride's story has always been fascinating—and inspirational.

A brilliant physics student at a top girls' high school (Westlake, now Harvard Westlake, in Los Angeles) and at Stanford, Ride's first ambition was to be a physics professor. She did that, and then became a champion of science education for children through her company, Sally Ride Science, which is still in business today.

But before all that, she became an astronaut and, in 1983, the first American woman in space.

Her NASA class of thirty-five future astronauts in 1978 was the first to include women. She told *Harvard Business Review* in 2012:

> "There was some culture shock, because they were used to male fighter pilots.... We spent a lot of time together, and that's where the camaraderie was built. We had a support system, and it didn't take very long for us to be accepted. That said, it was always comforting that there were six of us women, not two. It made it clear that NASA was committed to really bringing more gender diversity into the astronaut corps."

She often described herself as a "reluctant role model." As she told *HBR*:

> "I never went into physics or the astronaut corps to become a role model. But after my first flight, it became clear to me that I was one. And I began to understand the importance of that to people.
>
> "Young girls need to see role models in whatever careers they may choose, just so they can picture themselves doing those jobs someday. You can't be what you can't see."

Science was not the only domain in which she was expected to take a public stand. Her personal life was also fair game.

Ride spent most of her adult life with Tam O'Shaughnessy, whom she had known since they were both competing in girls' tennis tournaments in Southern California.

The two were partners in work as well as in life, building Sally Ride Science as a public company, of which O'Shaughnessy still serves as executive director.

Ride and O'Shaughnessy were private about their relationship for decades until 2011, when Ride was diagnosed with pancreatic cancer, the disease that took her life seventeen months later.

In 2017 O'Shaughnessy described their decision to wait to come out publicly:

> "The reason was simple," she told *HuffPost*. "Our company depended on corporate sponsorships, and back then we didn't have the confidence corporate leaders would support us if they knew we were a couple."

The world finally saw the whole Sally Ride after her death, when President Barack Obama awarded her the Presidential Medal of Freedom in 2013—and O'Shaughnessy became the first same-sex partner to accept the medal publicly at the White House.

Throughout my career in journalism, I have lived by the bedrock principle that "we are not the story." The people, events, and ideas we write about are infinitely more important than who we are and what we think. I still believe that. But now, as I enter a new phase of semiretirement, I also understand the value of letting readers hear my voice, telling my story in my own way.

You can be what you can see.

Thank you, Dr. Ride.

Amelia Earhart

By Angie Klink

Amelia Earhart had two quests that gained altitude at Purdue University: to encourage women to have careers and to soar the waistline of the world in a flying laboratory.

Purdue President Edward C. Elliott wanted professional women on the West Lafayette, Indiana, campus to attract more female students. When he and Earhart were speakers at the 1934 Women and the Changing World Conference in New York City, Earhart told Elliott that her primary interest in life was "the problem of careers for women." Elliott replied, "We want you at Purdue."

"I'd like that," Earhart said. "What do you think I should do?"

Earhart would spend several weeks a year as an aeronautics advisor and head Purdue's new Department for the Study of Careers for Women. Attracted to Purdue because it was the only university in the country with its own airport, Earhart was the first "Women's Career Counselor" at any university.

Earhart gave Depression-weary Americans hope. She arrived on campus in November 1935 holding twelve aviation records and had even taken Eleanor Roosevelt "skylarking" on an impromptu night flight.

Before Purdue's first women's career conference, "New Ideas in Education for Women," Earhart sent a questionnaire to female students about their plans after graduation to help them clarify their goals and help professors develop courses for women. Earhart also sketched notes for a "Handyman's Course," where female students would learn household repairs.

Women were not allowed to wear pants on campus. However, Earhart, who stayed in the Women's Residence Hall, came to dinner in her flying clothes. Students nervously watched, but she was not sent to her room to change.

A student recalled, "One night I was sitting in my room studying, and Miss Earhart stuck her head in the door and asked if she could borrow my pen. She said, 'I'll bring it back in a sec,' just like any girl would do. I guess I couldn't keep it to myself, because when she did bring it back, there was a bunch of girls in my room—just to get another look at her. But really, you know, I don't think she gets enough sleep. She's terribly busy. I often hear her typewriter clear up to midnight."

Earhart's husband, George Palmer Putnam, told Elliott that Earhart "was hankering for a bigger and better plane, not only one in which she could fly farther and faster and more safely, but to use as a laboratory for research in aviation education and for technical experimentation."

Earhart wanted to test human reactions to flying regarding diet and altitude, fatigue, and how men's and women's responses may differ. Elliott held a dinner party where Earhart spoke. By evening's end, two Purdue trustees donated about $40,000 toward the cost of Earhart's flying laboratory.

Earhart received her Lockheed Electra in California on her thirty-ninth birthday, July 24, 1936. "It's simply elegant," she said. "I could write poetry about this ship." In September she flew it to the Purdue Airport, where students greeted her. The mood on the Purdue campus must have been electric.

It was, in a sense, Purdue's plane. Purdue's Amelia. Purdue's world flight. She began her world flight in March.

However, Earhart crashed on takeoff in Honolulu, Hawaii. Once the plane was repaired, she reversed course and took off again from Miami on June 1, 1937. Elliott sent Putnam a telegram:

... GIVE A.E. A SPECIAL PURDUE GREETING WHEN SHE LANDS TODAY STOP HER COURAGEOUS EXPLOIT HAS GIVEN THRILL TO EVERY MEMBER OF THE BOILERMAKERS GUILD STOP THEY ARE ALL WITH HER TO THE SUCCESSFUL END OF THE FLIGHT

On July 2, Earhart's plane disappeared over the Pacific Ocean between Lae, New Guinea, and Howland Island.

She was writing a book titled *World Flight* and along her route had mailed her writings to her husband. When her plane vanished, Putnam already had a written account of his wife's journey; the book was retitled *Last Flight*.

Earhart penned, "Here was shining adventure, beckoning with new experiences, added knowledge of flying, of peoples—of myself. I felt that with the flight behind me I would be more useful to me and to the program we had planned at Purdue."

Two weeks after Earhart's plane went missing, Elliott sent a telegram to Putnam. "She would not want us to grieve and weep, yet we are in the deepest depths of sadness," he wrote. "We shall long mourn this gallant one whose life was a courageous adventure. She would have a heroine's part in any age."

Elliott was correct. Earhart continues to be a heroine in any age, an inspiration to all, but particularly for women as an example of focused bravery to follow one's quests.

Mary Emily Foy

By Nicole Catarino

The Los Angeles Public Library's first head librarian was a man who smoked jimsonweed in his office during public hours. LAPL's second head librarian was a painter whose excessive alcohol use caused him to miss enough shifts that the library board discharged him before the end of the year. In the face of their failures, a woman was considered, and the board appointed 18-year-old Mary Foy to the position. Rumors say this decision was done out of sympathy, as a show of good charity for her father's inability to support her. How generous, indeed.

"Are you the only man working here?" the woman asks, gesturing to my coworker. She cradles a stack of books under her arm, the ones I just slid back to her with a due slip attached. When he nods, she grins. "Boy, you must love having all these women over you—or under you!"

The four of us at the circulation desk cough out shocked laughs, smiles tight enough for my teeth to hurt. Said coworker looks like he would rather be swallowed up by one of the town's infamous potholes than sit here a second longer, caught between his obligation to teach me how to work our library's cataloging system and his understanding that fleeing the scene may give the rest of us reprieve. I'm suddenly hyper-aware of my outfit, the new dress and flats I'm freezing in, a harsh deviation from jeans and sneakers. The fabric itches where it's bunched around my crossed knees.

The woman leaves with one last laugh. My coworker whispers an abashed "sorry" under his breath, though I can't tell what he's apologizing for—sorry that happened; sorry you were here for it; sorry this is only your first day.

I exchange a look with the other two women next to me. They're unmoved. Used to it. So, then, this is what we do.

When the Los Angeles Public Library was first opened in 1872, women were forbidden to use it. Within six months, the policy changed. Women could use the library cards of male relatives to access the collections or sit in the book-less "Ladies Room" to peruse magazines. They were not allowed to hold their own cards.

In 1880 Mary Foy was appointed as the first female head librarian in the country. She created a catalog system out of the library's materials, and in her mind, so that she could find any book on the shelves in a matter of minutes. She refereed chess matches in the reading room and trivia bets raging in the downstairs saloon, and gained the respect of all her patrons. Still, she was not allowed to grant library cards to her fellow women. Manage information, never knowledge. Learn under someone else's thumb.

An older man walks into the library. He asks if there's anyone smart around to help him; when I raise my hand and offer assistance, he repeats the question.

"Are you smart?"

"I'm smart," I say. "How can I help you?"

He has a problem with his e-book account. I point him toward one of our head librarians. He tilts his head.

"I thought you were the smart one?" He drawls this with a smile. He's joking.

"I'm very smart," I answer quickly, with surprising confidence. "I just don't know that program well enough to help you."

My coworker does her best to solve his issue amidst his rough attempts at flirty humor and his insistence that he should tip her for her time. He leaves when his account works to his satisfaction and thanks us both for our kindness. My coworker raises her eyebrows at me when he's out of sight. *Could you believe that?*

"At least he was nice?" I offer. She rolls her eyes.

"These old men are all the same. They all think they're hilarious." Her smile appears. "See, you'll miss all the stories when you go into archiving."

The man's question bothers me for the rest of the day. "Are you smart?" Enough to help you? Enough to work here?

That afternoon, I help a woman register a library card for herself over the phone; later, her husband arrives to retrieve the books she asked me to hold, all checked out under her name.

Mary Foy was removed from her position in 1884 by the library board, despite her biting criticism. It was no use: Her father could now afford to support her.

When she passed away in 1962, LAPL created The Mary E. Foy California Room in her honor.

When the building was reconstructed in 1986, her name was nowhere to be found.

Louisa May Alcott

By Beth Welch

January 2, 202–

Dear Ms. Alcott,

Or Louisa, if I may? I feel I have known you since age eight, when my own dear mother introduced me to *Little Women* and took me on my first tour of Orchard House. How I identified back then with the novel's—and the docent's—plucky coming-of-age story, for I too was one of four sisters from a New England family with a literary bent and uneven economic fortunes. My nickname remains Beth, but of course I wanted to be Jo.

As did my eldest sister, Cathy, who of our quartet most resembled Jo. I write in part because she died two Decembers ago, in the midst of her favorite holiday season, and "Christmas doesn't seem Christmas" without her. Your scenes of Beth's decline and death are for me the most haunting of the novel, and I have turned often to them to connect with Cathy's spirit. Yes, she was "my conscience" in life, but I have only to return to her memorial bench, often with *Little Women* in hand, to pick up our conversation. Thank you for writing sisterhood so very well.

But I write mainly to report a profound disconnect between the scholarship on your work and life that flourishes well over a hundred years after your death and the tour of Orchard House that remains sunnily frozen in time, judging from the one I took last month, fifty-eight years after my first. My historian father frequently embarrassed me by calling out docents on factual errors, so I refrained from noting that you were born in Germantown, Pennsylvania, not Concord, Massachusetts. But I couldn't let the rosy picture of your father pass—yes, Bronson Alcott was an influential educational reformer who brought recess to the American school day and made you the vaunted shelf-desk on which you wrote your masterpiece, but I felt compelled to point out that Bronson's religious-fanatic ideals did not allow him to provide for his family, forcing your well-born mother to beg relatives for money and take on paying, often menial, work on top of raising a large family. Stark deprivation, not the patchy poverty of the March family, was your daily reality. And didn't your father construct that writing table not only to encourage your singular talent but also to insist that you add to the family's coffers?

The woodshed original to Orchard House is now the gift shop, and I exited it with the profound hope that my docent will start to read some of the excellent work on you and your family that continues to proliferate. As do discoveries of the fabulously Gothic stories credited to you early in your career! I cannot wait to read "The Phantom," penned by E. H. Gould, a Dickens-inspired Christmas tale in which the ghost is a woman. So Jo.

With love and admiration,

Elizabeth (Beth) Welch

January 6, 202–

Dear Ms. Welch,

Thank you for your note. I grew up accustomed to letters from my revered Ralph Waldo Emerson and Nathaniel Hawthorne, so your more personal mode of communication is revelatory, as is your address. Am I to assume that "Ms." is some amalgam of "Miss" and "Mrs." designed to disguise a woman's marital status? For my part, I was proud to refer to myself as a "literary spinster." Language should evolve and reflect its day, of course, but I happily reveled in my economic success as a single woman. I kept "my family cozy," and that was my life's major goal.

So please let the docents at Orchard House continue to tell the tale of *Little Women*. After all, thousands of admirers from around the world visit to hear the story of my life, and I have descendants to consider. I support, however, your desire to complicate it in an interesting way by bringing in good recent scholarship in an attractive manner—for example, by highlighting my nickname of Orchard house, "Apple Slump," and explaining its derivation.

We spirits do keep watch, and trust me, your dear and highly sociable Cathy visits me perhaps too often. She asks me to join you both on her bench in nearby Newburyport. May I assume such a union to be quite a memorable Christmas present?

Sincerely yours,

Louisa May Alcott

Vijaya Lakshmi Pandit

By Dimple Dhabalia

I come from a long lineage of fierce women. Their quiet strength and unwavering determination were the unspoken pillars that had held both sides of my family together for generations, providing the steadfast support and resilience needed to lead their families through the challenges of their time—colonization and occupation, racism, partition, independence, displacement, poverty, mental health issues, domestic violence, and more.

Despite this, since my childhood, my immersion into the rich history and culture of my ancestral homeland was grounded in selective narratives about the role that the "great men" of India played in securing India's independence from the British. Focusing on the contribution of men in history isn't unique to my family or my culture; however, the male-dominated lens through which our history was viewed ensured that like many other women of note from around the world, Vijaya Lakshmi Pandit remained out of my worldview for four decades of my life, until the summer of 2015. This was the summer I happened to travel to Pandit's birthplace, Allahabad, India, to scatter my maternal grandfather's ashes.

Pandit grew up with her older brother, Jawaharlal Nehru, and other siblings in a beautiful pale yellow mansion called Anand Bhavan. With wraparound white balconies, it reminded me of the Creole cottages in the French Quarter in New Orleans, but combined with the intricate carvings and domes common in Mughal architecture. Discovering Vijaya Lakshmi Pandit as I toured the home was a revelation for me. Her unwavering commitment to feminism and her

65

tireless advocacy for women's rights resonated deeply with my own journey as a woman navigating multiple cultures, identities, and roles in historically male-dominated professions.

Intrigued by the little I'd learned about her, I later Googled Pandit. The search yielded a respectable 3.8 million results, which left me frustrated that I'd gone my whole life not knowing about her. How could I search for someone I never *knew* to search for?

She'd spent her early life in the shadow of prominent men like Mahatma Gandhi and Sardar Vallabhbhai Patel, who alongside Nehru were considered fathers of the Indian independence movement and credited with unyoking India from her British oppressors. Pandit and several other women had been in the same rooms as these men. Like these men, these women had been arrested on multiple occasions for their resistance to British occupation, and they had played a far more significant role than the men in the development of a constitution. Through their collective efforts they ensured women would have rights in a postcolonial India. Yet they and their extraordinary contributions have shown up as nothing more than minor footnotes in history, while men's accomplishments have been documented and celebrated.

Pandit's remarkable political trajectory, starting with her role as the first Indian woman to serve in a cabinet position in pre-independent India, over time transitioned into numerous successes in the diplomatic service. She served as ambassador to the Soviet Union, United States, Mexico, and Spain—countries vital to the success of the social and economic status of the fledgling country as it tried to find its postindependence footing. She was also entrusted with the role of ambassador to Ireland and high commissioner to the United Kingdom. For twenty-two years she headed the Indian delegation to the United Nations, including one year as the first female president of the United Nations General Assembly.

However, despite her numerous professional successes, it was ultimately Pandit's femininity that the British patriarchy most feared—similar to the fear we witness today as the patriarchy fights to maintain its foothold in a modern world.

At the stroke of midnight on August 15, 1947, India's struggle for freedom culminated in the birth of a new nation, marking a turning point in the country's history and the beginning of a new era of self-governance and sovereignty. As an anti-colonialist, Pandit's symbolic value as a woman who possessed political savvy, diplomatic prowess, and the ability to effectively navigate the all-male bureaucratic spaces in which she operated, ran contrary to the imperialist propaganda of the subjugated Indian woman the British had used to justify its occupation of India for almost a century. She was proof of India's ability to self-govern—a daughter of India who embodied the aspirations and dreams of a nation ready to stand on its own.

Sonia Sotomayor

By Lara N. Dotson-Renta

"Home is the place that you believe you belong to." Sonia Sotomayor (Bronx Children's Museum video, 2020.)

Sonia Sotomayor became a Supreme Court justice in 2009, the year my eldest daughter was born. Sotomayor was sworn in with her *mami* holding the family Bible, no doubt marked up by an *abuelita*'s steady hand. I had never felt so Puerto Rican and, for perhaps the first time, so "American."

That summer, the newly appointed Justice Sotomayor posed on the cover of *Latina* magazine, fierce red nails front and center. Although she was featured on numerous magazine covers, this one stood out. In her black judicial robes, she looked directly at *us*; with one hand on her lap and another prominently on her chest, her pose showcased the classic red nails so recognizable to me and many Latinas.

Given the advice to wear neutral shades to confirmation hearings lest she be viewed as distracting, Sotomayor heeded until the reception held for her by then President Obama, at which she appeared in red nails. The message at the reception and on the cover was one of normalization, that you can wear something coded as "Latina" and still be deemed authoritative. You can take up the most revered intellectual spaces as you are, and not play the role as someone else. Then and now, many of us took notice.

For those of us of a certain era and background, Sonia Sotomayor played a unique role in our perception of ourselves and our dreams of possibility. I was in elementary school when we left Puerto Rico for the US mainland, joining generations before us that have existed in the "*vaivén*" (the coming and going) between our small island and the States. Justice Sotomayor's pattern of speech and her references to growing up in the Bronx felt intimate and tangible. The fact that she never sought to elide her working-class origins but rather took pride in them was significant to those of us who grew up straddled between places, carrying on our backs the dreams of our mothers and grandmothers, spread among broken languages and faded photographs.

As a young doctoral student subsumed in new motherhood and swallowed by what I didn't yet understand was postpartum depression, I was transfixed by her poise. She, like me, had struggled with chronic illness since childhood—for her, diabetes; for me, epilepsy. Exhausted, I watched, rapt, as Justice Sotomayor gave texture to her trajectory, context to her history and future. She was clearly a brilliantly accomplished woman. Yet embedded in some of the commentary was a latent questioning of whether someone with her background "belonged" on the Supreme Court. I recognized the well-practiced effort of proving that you belong in her even-keeled answers and demeanor. I wondered if my own daughter would one day feel the need to negotiate who she was in light of how she was perceived.

I thought back to the stinging loneliness of my first week at college, when I was asked if I might only be half Puerto Rican, since I didn't "seem like those people." For better or worse, the question lit a fire inside of me—the kind that burns slowly, passionately. I wondered if Justice Sotomayor felt the same under the world's attention, if she ever struggled locating "home."

I watched Sonia Sotomayor get sworn in live. I called my grandmother in Puerto Rico so we could watch in unison. Standing by her mother and brother in a soft white suit, the new Supreme Court justice said, "I, Sonia Sotomayor, do solemnly swear ..." She didn't anglicize her name, but rather said it as she had heard it her whole life. The accent was a bridge from Puerto Rico and from the Bronx to the halls of Washington, DC, an articulation of her aspirations and those of so many like her. I imagined the prayers whispered into that family Bible over the years coming to fruition, a *bendición* (blessing) of effort realized. The shifting cadence of Sotomayor's voice unapologetically claimed her space on the highest court of the land, as a Puerto Rican and as an "American."

When I received my doctoral degree in 2011, I brought my daughter up with me, because you have to "see it to imagine it."

Today my daughter is in high school. She is interested in the law.

Margarethe von Trotta

By Pamela Katz

Most of my extended family wallows in our tragic past. A few of us ran for the hills. Me? I ran like hell and was still running until I finally discovered a middle path. That didn't happen until I was over 40 and began working with the legendary filmmaker, Margarethe von Trotta.

It started in 1999. The phone rang and I was stunned to hear the voice of my favorite director, calling to ask if I'd like to work with her on a screenplay. It was the offer of a lifetime.

The script was for *Rosenstrasse,* a story about German women who risked their lives to protest the deportation of their Jewish husbands. Margarethe wanted a contemporary element and asked me to provide an authentic Jewish American perspective. Since my parents were firmly on the running side of the family, our cultural heritage had consisted of a shortened Seder, whose story seemed very far away, and a Chanukah with eight candles because some ancient tribe ran out of oil. How could I ever be Jewish enough to help write Margarethe's film?

My father was a Jewish émigré who left Germany when he was 17. My mother was from an orthodox household in Brooklyn. They were both determined to raise me and my sisters as hopeful Americans: *Don't raise children in fear. Don't let them identify as victims.* My father told us nothing about his agonizing escape as a teenager; my mother protected me from the gruesome stories others in his family often repeated. My parents hoped their silence would give me a clean slate. Neither of them realized there's no such thing.

When Margarethe and I met at Starbucks in midtown Manhattan, I proposed that the contemporary perspective of secular New York Jews would be a better parallel for the assimilated Jews in wartime Berlin. What a relief when she agreed! That was a world I knew.

Margarethe showed me the Rosenstrasse ("street of Roses") where the women looked down the barrels of the Nazi's guns and shouted "Give us back our husbands." I showed her the secular Jewish capital of the world: New York's Upper West Side.

One of the main characters in the script had been a child on the Rosenstrasse. Her mother was murdered and her Aryan father abandoned her. She immigrated to New York and tried to forget her past. The film begins when her husband suddenly dies and her long-repressed memories come back with force. Her adult children are stunned when she insists on a religious shiva, demanding rules and rituals they knew nothing about.

Margarethe had many questions: What do the shiva stools look like? Does everyone take a month off, go barefoot, and stop shaving? I had no answers. In my family, you got together after work and ate and talked and wept. Shoes on, mirrors uncovered, no rituals at all. Soon, Margarethe was teaching me about the Jewish traditions we'd never practiced. She even enjoyed the irony, although she was astonished to see how deliberately I had avoided my father's painful past. Her astonishment demanded an answer. For the script but, far more importantly, for me.

In order to create the other main character, a daughter determined to find out what her mother experienced during the war, I had to portray someone far braver than I had ever been. I had no choice but to follow in the fictional daughter's footsteps—and finally seek the truth my father had buried.

It has taken me too long to accept that I was defined, as everyone is, by a past that began before I was born. I'd refused to admit that the air I breathed was filled with my father's fear, and shame, and his complex gratitude. He'd won back a right I had never had to question: the right to live. That was the gap between us, one that never closed. That air was mixed with my mother's American Jewish optimism, her determination to shield us from his nightmares. It would be thanks to her that I had an innocent childhood, but it was Margarethe, a German director who devoted her life and films to the history of her country, who taught me that there's no future without understanding the burdens of one's past. She showed me a path hidden in the darkness, and promised me I would find myself, a far better self, on the other side.

Thank you, Margarethe, not only for the professional opportunity but also for the personal gift—of a lifetime.

Jessica Mitford

By Mimi Pond

Who were the Mitford Sisters? The short answer is this: They were women who did a bunch of shit they weren't supposed to do. Born to a minor member of the aristocracy in the early years of the twentieth century, they were raised in isolation in England's Cotswolds' District. Their parents were essentially Victorians who would grudgingly live out their lives in the modern world. As such, David Freeman-Mitford, second Baron Redesdale, did not believe in educating girls. Isolated in the middle of nowhere, the sisters got only a rudimentary education at home from tutors.

No one resented this more than Jessica, the fifth of six sisters, born in 1917. If David Mitford and his wife thought they were raising daughters who would dutifully marry into the aristocracy and pump out aristocratic children, well, they had a big surprise coming. Eldest sister, Nancy (born in 1904), who would go on to become a wildly successful comic novelist with books like *The Pursuit of Love*, was in charge of cracking the jokes and set the comedy bar very, very high. The three other older sisters were Pam, Diana, and Unity, with one brother, Tom. There would be one more sister, Deborah (Debo), born in 1920.

Diana married first, at nineteen (anything to get out of the house), but scandalously bolted two children and three years later to be mistress and later wife of Oswald Mosley, head of the British Union of Fascists. Inspired, teenaged Unity declared her love for fascism and vowed to meet Adolf Hitler. Contrarily, Jessica declared herself a Communist at twelve and started her own "running away" fund at Drummond's

Bank. Debo vowed to marry a duke. Here's the interesting thing: These sisters ALL DID EXACTLY WHAT THEY SAID THEY WERE GOING TO DO.

Unity later successfully stalked and became dear friends with the Führer, which did not end well. Diana remained a staunch fascist until the end of her life. Debo married the younger son of a duke, but when his brother died in World War II, he and she became the Duke and Duchess of Devonshire. Jessica took her running away fund and bolted at nineteen to cover the Spanish Civil War as a journalist with her rebellious teenaged cousin (and later husband) Esmond Romilly. She was Winston Churchill's cousin; he was Churchill's nephew. Later, Jessica would become a full-fledged Communist, an American civil rights and union rights activist, and, after that, a best-selling memoirist, muckraking journalist, and, briefly, late in life, a punk rocker.

Of course I didn't know any of this when I was seven years old and my parents checked a new bestseller out of the library in the spring of 1963 called *The American Way of Death* by Jessica Mitford. My parents wouldn't stop raving about this engaging and very funny book, all about how corrupt the American funeral industry was. It was so clever, so witty, so scathing, and of course it was about essentially one of their favorite topics: how "they" were always out to get you! It was all a con! It wasn't that they were wild radicals. They'd witnessed their parents struggle through the Great Depression and, as God was their witness, they'd never pay full retail for anything! Because of this book, they joined a local funeral society and, as a result, my mother saved *90 percent* on the cost of her own cremation, thrilling her beyond the grave.

I had no idea until my mid-20s, when a friend said to me, "You know, she had sisters," that there was more than one Mitford. After that they became, more and more obsessively, my hobby. What I finally realized was that the sisters—all of them, for better or for worse—managed to embody everything about the twentieth century. But my money was always on Jessica.

Jessica managed to do it all. Being blood-related to the Churchills, fighting Franco, meeting Katharine Graham (née Meyer) of the *Washington Post* when she was still a debutante, losing her husband, Esmond, to WWII, fighting for civil rights in Mississippi and Alabama, interviewing William Faulkner, battling the HUAC (House Un-American Activities Committee), writing a book about the trial of Dr. Benjamin Spock, hosting fundraising parties for the Black Panthers (her second husband was their lawyer) with guests like Jean Genet, and becoming solid BFFs with Maya Angelou.

More than anything, though, through much heartbreak and tragedy, with humor as her weapon, Jessica Mitford just kept going.

Taylor Swift

By Julia Totten and Laura Rossi-Totten

How and why did Taylor Swift become an essential part of our mother-daughter relationship?

Song #1: "Begin Again"

Laura

Our Swift story begins in 2013. You were 10, I was 43, and Taylor Swift was 24. I thought you would grow out of Taylor Swift and, by default, I would too, but I simply had to take you to your first concert. The artist wasn't terribly important—! Hyper, happy, anxious, expectant, I knew the night would be amazing. As Taylor sings "We are alone with our changing minds," but even so, I always knew you and I would share this special moment.

Song #2: "State of Grace"

Julia

I have a secret: I liked Taylor's music, but I wasn't super-invested before the Red concert. I'd always wanted to go to a big stadium concert with you. Yet that evening became a core life memory: my first concert, my special experience with my mom, and my introduction to Taylor Swift, now one of my favorite artists.

Song #3: "You Belong with Me"

Laura

Do you remember that night? Rain, wind, then the most spectacular sunset? The electrifying sense of instant community? Our seats were close to the last row in the stadium. We were surrounded by mothers and daughters. Maybe it's because her lyrics connect us: Moms time-travel back to our own meaningful firsts—first best friend, first love, first heartbreak—while simultaneously offering a glimpse of those same first milestones to our daughters. We yearn in unity. Together we felt the power of Taylor's opening line of "Love Story": "We were both young when I first saw you," with one of us looking forward (you), one of us looking back (me).

Song #4: "Love Story"

Julia

The nosebleed seats didn't matter. What mattered was that I could sing along with thousands of strangers in a stadium. We all knew the words. We could all sing *with* Swift. I especially loved singing the part of "We Are Never Getting Back Together" where Swift imitates a phone call: "Ugh, so he calls me up and he's like, 'I still love you.' And I'm like, 'I just, I mean, this is exhausting, you know? Like, we are never getting back together, like, ever'" I loved Taylor's sassiness, and I loved playing the little part she created along with everyone else in the stadium.

Song #5: "We Are Never Getting Back Together"

Laura

Here's *my* secret: When you made plans to go to the 2023 Eras concert at the same stadium without me, I was surprised by the sadness I felt when I realized you were independent enough to go on your own. That realization hit me hard because sometimes (OK, a lot!) I want to freeze time and tell you to "Never Grow Up."

Song #6: "Never Grow Up"

Julia

Mom, I missed you, even though I had a terrific time with my best friend. The echoes of Red were right there. In "August," Swift tells us how "August slipped away into a moment in time" ... I felt our younger selves alongside me. Swift is part of our bond—providing an example of a powerful woman that has progressed in her life just as my mom and I have. We have always loved her music and her success, always texting each other songs, pictures, and articles; Swift is a favorite topic, a mutual friend.

Song #7: "August"

Laura

We're in sync! When I watched the Eras concert movie without you, I knew we both experienced things as we were meant to—not together, yet still shared. Taylor teaches us that whether it's love, heartbreak, growing up, or growing old, together and apart, that "Everything will be alright." As I'm typing this, neither of us is 22, but we can both scream our favorite lyrics: "We're happy, free, confused, and lonely at the same time.... It's miserable and magical"—and it's as if we're both back at that first concert, but better.

Song #8: "22"

Julia

Swift symbolizes my evolution. Her song "Fifteen" reminds me of this—she sings how "when you're fifteen feeling like there's nothing to figure out" and how fifteen is "life before you know who you're gonna be." My 10-year-old and 21-year-old selves look at these lyrics very differently. When I was 10, I could barely conceptualize being 15, let alone understand who I would be at 21. Now I look back and know exactly what Swift meant—I didn't have a care in the world beyond my day-to-day life. At 21 there are many things to figure out. Swift's music showcases the passage of time in a way that offers complex perspectives for all generations. Through my own lens, I can see how I have grown up—and then imagine the experience through my mom's eyes too.

Song #9: "Fifteen"

Julia and Laura
Thanks, Taylor.
Song #10: "Lover"

Jane Smiley

By Krisela Karaja

Why does a daughter hate? Jane Smiley poses this question to me in high school during my first reading of her novel *A Thousand Acres*. A retelling of Shakespeare's *King Lear* from one of the "bad" daughters' perspectives, Smiley's character, Ginny Cook Smith, would answer the question tragically: because her father sexually abused her and her sister.

My answer is thankfully far less tragic; my father is no monster, no Larry Cook. In most respects he's a good dad: He's brought my sister and me to the United States from formerly communist Albania, he encourages us to focus on our education, and he's already paid off our family home.

I see myself reflected in Ginny, whose mother, like mine, died when Ginny was young. I see parallels between our families' obsession with land: the Cooks on farming it and my family on a raised ranch on a half-acre of US soil, as my father was cheated of full ownership of his childhood home.

While I do not see direct parallels between my father and Larry, I hear sound bites echoing Larry's razor-sharp tongue in my dad. At 17, I hate my father in these moments of grief, when he retreats into what Smiley terms an "impenetrable fog of self" over the death of my mother—and *right after we purchased the house*. He laments being a single dad in a foreign country, without the female anchor that many men of his generation require. He regresses into his six-year-old self, overhearing his older brothers calling his pregnant sisters *whores* as they press the girls to reveal their lovers or rapists. In moments of frustration, my father unknowingly resurrects these ghosts and gives them life in our home, forty years later, retelling his past in our present.

When I'm not drying the dishes fast enough—his 80-year-old mother could dry them faster—and I retort that I'm working as fast as I can, or I put down the towel and tell him to dry his own damn dishes, suddenly I'm a *duarë-thatë* ("dry-handed," "lazy") *qene* ("dog"). Or I'll accept a ride from my neighboring classmate's aunt to a volunteer event and will surely be a *zuskë* ("slut") who's having an affair. Or I'll be majoring in English in college and am *e humbur*, a "loser" who is *mosmirënjohës* ("ungrateful") for his immigration. Or I'm just a *bad daughter* who will abandon him when he's older.

At 17 I believe myself a *kafshë*, an "animal," when I yell back because why would a *good daughter* hate the father she loves when she knows his why, when she has the capacity to see his psychological layers?

At 17 Jane Smiley tells me that I'm no beast; I'm just a girl who needs to be seen, and I love her like a mother for it.

Why does a daughter hate? Because she can. Smiley plants the seed of unabashed female fury in me. If Ginny, engulfed in her own *impenetrable fog of self*, can attempt to poison her sister, then I can certainly accept my ire toward my father.

Smiley's seed of anger grows in my 20s when I spend a depressive year self-confined at home, my rage a roaring twister whirling faster than my father's own tempests. This year is my salvation: Like Smiley, I apply to master of fine arts programs. I storm on the page.

This resentment is rarer now, in my 30s. My father is aging and, through self-fulfilling prophecy, is isolated in his raised ranch razed of daughters, lamenting his *bad luck*. His sincere apologies—and distance—have brought us closer. It is easier to love now. Yet, having spent most of my 20s fleeing his home, I am wary of returning. I don't want the house bulldozed, as is the fate of the Cooks' Chelsea model; I'll settle for a sale. Yet to mention selling the house and its half-acre, my father's legacy and Achilles' heel, is blasphemy.

My anger is no longer taboo; it no longer possesses me. When it arises, I embrace the unabashed part of it—cradle it as Ginny does her own *gleaming obsidian shard.* By caressing my fury, I lessen its hold, and only then do I dream: Father's Day in a modest condo and my two future daughters joking in Albanian with their grandpa, who lives next door. I smile. Thank you, Jane.

Sandra Cisneros

By Katherine Duarte

To: Sandra Cisneros   Cc Bcc

Subject: Keep a Lookout for My Name

Dear Miss Cisneros,

How is San Miguel de Allende treating you? I read online that you
sold your pink house a few years back. How sad! I was hoping you'd
invite me for some coffee (though I have a certain preference for Cafe
Presto or Juan Valdez, since American makes me sick). Don't worry,
though, I'm sure we can make something work.

I'm working on a book about my mother, her mother, my *abuela*'s
mother, my great-*abuela*'s mother, and any other mothers I end up discovering along the way. I don't know when that book will be published
but, between you and me, it probably won't be seen on the shelf for
a while, because I have yet to cure this terrible disease of mine called
overthinking. You see, this story is important to me. It's about my
family, my culture, my language; about Latinidad, about immigrants,
about Latin-Americans, about folks like you and me.

It's a book about girls: *A las Mujeres. To the Woman.* I'm sure you
understand. Growing up Chicana, you learned that Latina women
resided in an entirely different world than men, one defined by traditional cultural codes and gendered expectations of marriage, the image
of the mother like an all-seeing eye over our every move. Did we have
to learn to grow up fast, or did growing up fast force us to learn? This
is how it must have been for Esperanza when she wore those magic
shoes, feeling beautiful until beautiful hurt.

Do you happen to know if Mamacita ever made it out of Mango Street? She reminds me of my mother. *No speak English.* All she ever talks about is going back to Nicaragua. There, we have a big house with a big pool in the backyard. Everybody calls her *Doña* Elizabeth, and she doesn't have to use Google Maps to get around or Google Translate to talk to her boss at the hotel. Nicaragua is her home, she says, not this country with the strange language. It is all she talks about. Everything here is slums and ghettos because there is *no hay suficiente dinero.* Sometimes I wonder if Nicaragua is why. She buys these big barrels to fill with shoes, and lights, and stuff we can't use because she sends it all to the big house. I tell her our home *is* here, but she does not listen. Did Mamacita do the same?

I want to tell stories as good as you who taught me that English and Spanish could coexist, how writing doesn't mean limiting myself to one language because I am afraid of getting lost in the other. This is what it means to be a Latin American writer: learning how to travel between two literary cultures. You take inspiration from memories of your childhood and people, weaving them into cities and characters for the next generation of readers to know what it is like to live differently. To read about Esperanza, Mamacita, ugly daughters, annoying sisters, is to see a reflection of my own life growing up on Mango Street, the people that make up my stories.

I hope that when we meet, perhaps for a cup of coffee, you can give me a tip or two about curing my overthinking. Maybe after, I can bring you a copy of that book I have yet to publish and tell you which characters were in my neighborhood. But for now, keep a lookout for my name.

All the best,
A Wannabe Writer

Audre Lorde

By Nyanka Kizzy

There is an elegance to riding Black Unicorns. Few ever master the act. I watch her lean her figure into the wind, cutting through it like the truth cuts to the heart of things—efficient and sometimes soft. I watch the way her body whispers. It tells me there's no room for ugly lies here. There's no room for any lies here. There's no room to fold her Blackness. It's too mythical for folding and far too magical for disappearing.

She dismounts and I am there, arms outstretched to hold her tender hand. She smiles and I am sucked closer into her orbit. I want to taste that smile. I wonder if she'll let me.

"If you had to say one thing, what would you tell the world?"

I see her brain working. Her mind moves with a ballerina's elegance and strength. She thinks and I wait patiently, because you wait for women who ride Black Unicorns and whose pen can shift universes.

"I'd tell Black women everywhere to expand."

"Expand?"

"Yes, I want them to bloat. I want them to take up space. Unapologetically. I want them to swallow everything except pain. Eat the universe. EAT THE UNIVERSE and shit it out."

She pauses.

"The universe would be so lucky to be in the mouth of a Black woman."

"How does one eat the universe?"

She looks at me. I watch her brain do its dance again. "The first step is opening your mouth, silly."

She opens her mouth, and inside her is a welcoming black pit; home. I let her swallow me. I want to be a part of her eternally. Pray she does not shit me out. Pray instead that she absorbs me.

Her skin is not empty. Inside is a multitude of everythingness. Of pain, of beauty, of words, and words, of many many thoughts eloquently twisted and tied until they are an elaborate quilt of everything God could've ever fathomed and perhaps some things God never could. Blasphemous, perhaps, but such is the foundation of the House of Lorde.

I drag my hands across the sturdy walls that line her insides. They are built of something whimsical. Their magic speaks to me, and it tells me it's made of mystical matter—unicorn horns. They will last forever. I look up to see how the roof sparkles and wonder briefly how the inside of the roof could dazzle, and then I remember she has swallowed everything, and life has a special sheen when you aren't terrified of folding out of yourself.

I look left to see an elegant glass staircase. I let my hands drag slowly along the banister as I ascend. I try not to look down in case I get too dizzy. I stomp quite hard, wondering if I could break the glass with my foot, but I fail. The staircase is quite sturdy. The entire structure is quite sturdy, and I know that it was crafted by someone with incredible skill and nimble fingers. I kiss the floor at the top of the stairs, and it kisses me back and it is then that I know ...

This house will stand forever.

Notes from a Black Woman: Read "Future Promise" and "Solstice" by Audre Lorde and eat this story again.

Mary Shelley

By Mary Lasley

Most teenagers are romantics, but only some are Romantics. On mid-2010s Tumblr, the social media platform-of-choice for those too weird for Instagram, there dwelled a small cult of users who did nothing but circulate wild stories about the Romantic poets; it was here that I first read the story of Byron and the Shelleys at Lake Geneva, 1816. Cooped up inside by grim weather, Byron proposed that they write ghost stories to pass the time—and Mary Shelley, a teenage girl with my name, sat down and wrote *Frankenstein*.

I became obsessed. Their story was part of an ongoing myth—young artists careening through Europe, sparking scandal and dying before the party ended—and I memorized every sordid fact Tumblr had to offer. Mary Shelley lost her virginity in a graveyard. Percy Shelley listed his destination on a hotel registry as "hell." Byron once disappeared completely and was found a week later, drunk, in a Parisian gutter. Many of the stories were true, while others were exaggerated or even made up altogether, but I didn't mind; the holes in the story were what allowed me to creep in and pretend I was part of the fun. I dreamed of a parallel history where school was optional, adventure was everywhere, the world was easily scandalized, and—most importantly—I had friends. When my classmates posted pictures from parties I wasn't invited to, I opened Tumblr and chose grandiosity over self-pity. I wasn't at odds with my peers; I was at odds with time itself! I was a Romantic poet. I was a Byronic hero. I was meant for something better. I had to be.

Mary Shelley's adventure, by her own admission, started when she ran away with Percy. Mine began about two years into college. I met my friend Grace, who invited me to a party, and fantasy hurtled into reality with a teeth-rattling crash. In the spray of sparks and metal that followed, I found myself dancing in the woods, screaming at the top of a hill, getting knocked over in the mosh pit, and laughing like a crazed saint as my friends—my *friends!*—hauled me upright again. I never made it to Geneva, but I did make a pilgrimage to Lord Byron's estate during my summer abroad in England, where I bought two shot glasses in the gift shop and took a selfie with his portrait. *Are you proud of me yet, you mad, bad bastard?*

Part of the reason the Romantics remain fascinating is because so many of them died before their lives had the chance to get dull. Shelley drowned in a storm at sea at the age of 29; Byron died a few years later of a fever in Greece. I was so afraid of graduating college that I'd slip away from parties to cry into the bathroom sink. I certainly never wanted to die young, but I also never shook my teenage habit of viewing life as a story—and there were moments at the end of senior year, sprawling over Grace's shoulder in a sweaty basement while our friends' bands shook the room, when I thought, *This might not be the worst note to go out on.* Maybe the room would keep getting hotter and the music would keep getting louder and the crowd would choke itself tighter and tighter until we all spontaneously combusted—absorbed into the atmosphere, floating around like glitter for the rest of eternity, while real life lurched along beneath us.

Mary Shelley, though, outlived the Romantic period. She outlived a lot of things. During my mania in high school, I'd largely ignored her later life, just as I'd disregarded Shelley's ill health and Byron's more jarring displays of nastiness. I never wondered what happened to her after the party started to wind down, leaving her in London with an infant son and her dead husband's heart wrapped in paper in her desk. It was more fun to imagine her as a disaffected teenager, helping me dye my hair blue, sitting next to me while I tore up my jeans and wrote poems on the rubber soles of my sneakers. Now, working at a coffee shop in my hometown six hours away from Grace, I realize that Mary Shelley is with me still.

I ask her, "What do you do when your story is over?"

"Write another one," she says.

Mary Oliver

By Rory Monaco

"I am so distant from the hope of myself,
In which I have goodness, and discernment,
And never hurry through the world
But walk slowly, and bow often.
Around me the trees stir in their leaves
And call out, "Stay awhile."
—Mary Oliver, "When I Am Among the Trees"

I crouch, palms pressing into the recently rained-upon soil, picking my hands up and seeing the handprint I've left. Chin resting on knees and knees tucked into my chest, I bow my head. My hands spread open on the tender earth, waiting for the weight of the world to hit.

A few seconds pass. A drop of rain slips off the leaves and onto my head. I timber backward, arms outstretched above my head, letting the soil soak my backside as I press flush against the ground. I know my hair will be crusty with mud, but that doesn't bother me. How much closer can I get? How much longer until the soil recognizes me as its own and rids itself of the barriers separating us?

My mind wanders to when I sit on the floor beside my bed, watching the doorknob jiggle as she tried and tried to open it. I silently cried while I had my godmother on the phone, listening to everything despite neither of us saying a word. It was important she was there, in case anything happened.

What could've set her off? I thought I'd been good recently. Sometimes I can snap back, tired of the words she spits at me, but I felt I'd been cautious recently. Aware of what to say and, more importantly, what not to say that could trigger her.

Her fist hit the door again. Despite my hands clamped over my ears, words slipped through the cracks of my fingers. "Bitch" and "selfish" made their way in, sinking into bone and flesh, becoming a part of my identity that I'd spend years trying to rid myself of.

I did something selfish recently? It's the first semester back online for school. Maybe I've been spending too much time on schoolwork and not enough with her? Could she think I'm ignoring her when I'm really just studying?

"I don't know any other daughters who lock their moms out of their rooms." I think that was the sound of a key jiggling in the lock. My pulse quickened. I texted my godmother that she might come in.

The wind whispers and ripples through the trees surrounding me. One leaf falls: a parachute to the acorn attached as it lands beside my foot. It could've come from any number of trees. I guess I should thank each and every one, rather than skipping over any. I picked the acorn up, smooth like a new book's pressed pages. Turned to show the acorn what one day it might grow into.

I began going on walks through the woods, figuring I ought to know what life looked like away from the four walls of my bedroom; I went as a guest. *I'm here to learn*, I spoke silently. *You cast shadows when plants beneath you need shade. You drop leaves when light is scarce and we all want the sunlight to fall on us. I am here, asking you for light. Show me a beautiful thing. Give me something to hold onto. I am dark and heavy. What if, one day, the soil beneath me can't bear this weight?*

I read that Mary Oliver wondered if the woods began to know her. Not as an individual, but perhaps in her presence. When her energy made its way into the forest, maybe something would shift. They knew not that she was herself, but that she wasn't another cardinal, nor an inkberry bush. She came with her own burdens and sought solace in their silence.

Now I'm here, wondering if these trees know me. Could tell that I might mimic their patterns of letting light seep in.

A worm slithers onto my leg. They always come crawling during a rainstorm. Why do I curl into myself once the sky starts to pour? I could learn a thing or two from them. Next time I'll join the worm, let him know he's not alone. I too enjoy stepping out into the pouring rain, if only to feel the mud splash as I spin and twirl.

Georgia O'Keeffe

By Kelley Gifford

Birch and Pine Trees No. 1, 1925

My third eye has frozen over in the back seat of a minivan. Images of unlucky children stuck in place until the thaw, tongues welded to frozen metal, oblige me to check if my forehead has become one with the car window. It hasn't.

So again I lean against the glass, gazing at the forest beside the road. If I narrow my focus, each leaf and pine needle stands in sharp relief. If I don't, a single brushstroke captures them all.

Out the opposite window, the forest continues as if a sea parted. As if at any moment it might collapse together, reuniting in the wake of humankind.

A Black Bird with Snow-Covered Red Hills, 1946

For me, remembering is like walking in footprints made by another person's shoes, adopting a goofy little hop to match their stride. This task takes too much focus, and I can't afford to look up to see whose lead I follow. One misstep, one toe in undisturbed dirt, means unequivocal death by molten lava. I don't make the rules.

New footprints stack atop the old, like a descant over a melody. There are places where my smaller shoe has left the larger undisturbed, many more where they intertwine.

Sky Above Clouds IV, 1965

When we engage our senses, we sacrifice a part of ourselves and offer it to the world, asking that it give our wounds the time to heal. We give it the power to break our hearts, and hope that the risk is worth it.

If we're lucky, we'll choose (or be chosen by) a passion to which we can give ourselves over, laying down slivers of our humanity like layers of mica until we've created something wholly new. In practice, this process is much less romantic. "It was a long trip with the brush across that twenty-four feet of canvas" says Georgia O'Keeffe of creating *Sky Above Clouds IV*, "once with water, twice with glue, and twice with white paint to prepare it. And then I had to paint the picture."

But the rest of us are confronted all at once with the full force of her passion. The artist shows us the infinite possibilities contained within a single perspective, and, in return, we feel her stare into our soul. The different shapes we may see in her clouds only confirm them as such, for is it not possible to look at the sky and see a lion chase a pair of scissors across the troposphere?

Her clouds are clouds because they might also be plant cells, perhaps of one of O'Keeffe's famous flowers, or a maze of icebergs, or an array of pillows. They're vertical and at the same time horizontal, a stone wall and a carefully laid walkway.

Antelope, 1954

She finds candles in the fourth drawer she checks. She lays them flat atop the counter and, after careful inspection, selects the four least melted. Four candles, fourth drawer. Her youngest son turns 4 tomorrow. This must be some kind of sign. She decides it's an auspicious one.

Just ten minutes have passed since the cake went into the oven, and the scent of vanilla already filters through the kitchen. She brings in the typewriter from the next room and finds that the smell has left every surface coated in a sweet layer of film.

She types the date, "1963," and the greeting: "Dear Mrs. Stieglitz."

She had first come across O'Keeffe's work three years ago in the *Time* feature "Wonderful Emptiness." Three paintings covered just a page and a half. Her throat tickled for a week after she saw them, and her gut twisted like a guilty conscience. So she cut them out, pinned them to her bulletin board, and was cured.

The paintings hang there still, amidst "notices from the dentist and the PTA." Every so often she rescues them from beneath grocery lists and Christmas cards. These little fragments of art have woven their way into her life and proven that her life is similarly a work of art.

At some point she had wanted to own an original O'Keeffe, but gave up soon after realizing she was famous. But of countless reproductions, only one copy of *Antelope* has been clipped by her hands. And so only this copy can make her feel as she does tonight, "after a hard day when the little boys drop off to sleep unexpectedly, and all is quiet."

Erma Bombeck

By Bonnie Jean Feldkamp

My mom died in a car accident when I was 7 years old. All of her secrets and womanly advice disappeared with her.

Erma Bombeck showed up in my life right on time. My daughter had just been born and I was figuring out what my life was going to look like. I desperately wanted to get this motherhood thing right. Erma was there to show me there was no such thing, and then together we laughed. Her columns were syndicated from 1965 to 1996, but I found her books in the library and many more of her columns on the internet.

Her voice shrugged off perfectionism, and her stories of motherhood made me feel as if I had stolen a glimpse into the secret world I'd been longing to understand. Erma showed me what womanhood in the 1970s and 1980s must have been like for my mom.

Erma served on President Carter's National Advisory Committee on Women. Jimmy Carter was the only Democrat my father voted for, which means my mom likely did too. Erma Bombeck joined Bella Abzug, Gloria Steinem, and Liz Carpenter for two years to champion the Equal Rights Amendment. Something Erma said, "may be the most misunderstood words since 'one size fits all.'"

The ERA failed to meet the requisite number of state ratifications by Congress's deadline of June 30, 1982, so it was not adopted as a constitutional amendment.

While Bombeck traveled the country championing equal rights, my mother, with three biological children and three foster children, traversed our neighborhood, volunteering for the 1980 census. I'd like to think they shared a certain grit. Fortitude seemed part of their DNA, and both Erma and my mother used their talents to make a difference in their respective communities.

I too yearn to make a difference in my community, and like Erma my medium is newspaper columns. As the opinion editor of the *Louisville Courier Journal*, I write the stories of our city through the lens of everyday people. I tie personal experience to current events, hoping readers will empathize, relate, and care. I want our children to know where they come from, and these stories, like my mother's, matter.

When my mom died, the photo of the smashed-up Toyota she was a passenger in made the front page of our local newspaper. Her story had been reduced to a cutline—just her name mentioned in the caption under the photo used to illustrate the dangers of ice on winter highways. Mom deserved better, and in some ways Erma's columns gave her story—the story of every ordinary woman—a voice.

Erma's columns detailed the struggles of motherhood in her generation, and she did it with wit, substance, and the sense that we were in this together. Before "mommy bloggers" there was Erma. She wrote about defrosting frozen ground beef under her arm for a last-minute dinner and about losing her glasses because she shoved them in a book somewhere to mark the page. I could see my mother in these details, and I could also see myself. That was the magic. We all roared with laughter because we could relate. Erma's humor wasn't the biting sarcasm of today's social media. Erma's humor had heart. Her columns about loving her stepfather and losing a child late in pregnancy are gut-wrenching, poignant, and brave.

Most important, her words offered the belonging I so craved. We're in this world together, after all, and Erma Bombeck knew exactly what that meant.

Patti LaBelle

By Patricia Wynn Brown

Have you ever had people who act as saboteurs of your success, ones who attempt to undermine you with petty gossip, backhanded compliments, or who pull the curtains down on your shining moments?

Patti LaBelle, R&B singer, musical genius, and star performer, tells us about her would-be detractors in her 1996 autobiography. Born Patricia Louise Holt in 1944 in East Philadelphia, she describes her hard-won rise to fame, taking us along for the marvelous ascent, but making sure we know it included those who would have halted her rise.

These incidents, which never stopped her, included a premature curtain call and a left-hook telegram.

When, for example, LaBelle's rendition of Dinah Washington's "Where Are You?" brought the house down one evening when she was performing alongside megastar James Brown, it so inflamed the more famous singer that he did something unthinkable: Brown brought down the stage curtains just as LaBelle was mid her triumphant bow.

That performance must have been quite an event: LaBelle even received a message from Dinah Washington herself. LaBelle tells her readers, "I was thrilled! ... The Queen of Blues had heard me!"

Once LaBelle read the telegram, however, the thrill was gone. "Stop singing my damned song" was what Washington commanded.

Jealousy is not uncommon. As a writer and performer, I've felt it many times, and it doesn't get easier. Someone else's poisonous envy can easily upturn my apple cart of confidence.

But then again, I am fortunate: I also have people who believe in me.

Those who believe in one's talent and skill can offer encouragement, support, applause, and approval when the moment is magic. Some people come into our lives and expand our horizons of possibilities, while others work like shrink-wrap to stifle our dreams.

Patti LaBelle cast a magic spell on me, cracking open my world.

LaBelle, a shy and self-doubting child, had to be bribed by her mother to leave the house. She wrote: "I saw myself as an ugly little black girl without much going for her." She had great support from her mom and dad. She said her dad made her "feel like a star." They would sit on the porch and sing songs. Her confidence grew.

She chose the song "You'll Never Walk Alone" at her first singing contest and won. At her later performances, which she describes as "part concert, part revival, part confession, and part church," she becomes that loving parent singing with you on the porch, reassuring you that you are not alone.

We had the opportunity to see her live at an outdoor concert in 1999.

LaBelle sparkled under the lights from the stage. She commanded the space like Cleopatra on the Nile. We, her loyal subjects, lounged on picnic blankets under the starry summer night sky. LaBelle's voice soared as her long and painted fingernails reached up to the heavens.

In between songs, she spoke to us about valuing ourselves and being kind to each other.

Bouquets of flowers were laid at her feet.

Toward the end of the concert, my husband left our blanket of friends and headed to the restroom.

It was then, right then, that LaBelle began singing a great song to dance to and we all rose and grooved.

We were about fifteen rows of blankets back, and as LaBelle walked down from the stage and moved fabulously through the crowd, I was amazed that she stopped in front of me and then took my hand.

She began leading me back up to the stage until she and I both reached center stage. We were under the lights. Then LaBelle turned to me—still singing, still holding my hand—and I did a ballet-style bow, blowing her a kiss.

Then she said this, and it has carried me through some very tough times: "Never ever let anyone take that spirit away from you—and they will try."

I floated back and sat down, stunned. Why had she chosen me? Just then, my husband returned. Our friends gushed, "You will never guess what just happened!"

My husband knows and appreciates my enthusiasm and spirit. He asked, "Did Patti, this Patti, get up on that damned stage?"

I did. I was invited. I was touched by an angel.

LaBelle wrote in her autobiography: "When you inspire someone to reach into themselves, to reach their potential, they can't help but pass on that inspiration to so many others. It makes you immortal."

LaBelle bestowed on me an everlasting new attitude.

Toni Morrison

By Pascale Joachim

Can I tell you a secret?

I used to not like Black people. In fact, there was a time I nearly hated them. In defense of my younger self, how else could I react to realizing the skin I was born with was not enough to protect me from their unfailing ability to other?

I could never wrap my mind around what it was they felt they needed to defend. I didn't understand their need to test, their demand for proof of blackness; and because I didn't understand, I grew apprehensive. Almost fearful. I embraced clothes, shoes, music, movies, and TV, stupidly hoping I'd gain something I now know I never lacked. Finding you helped me understand and, eventually, forgive.

Can I tell you something else?

I first heard your name during my third year of college. I've always loved reading, but I could never connect with what I read. Until you, the finest literature was that of Fitzgerald, Camus, or Steinbeck. Woolf or Chopin, if I was lucky. While quarantined, I realized how tired I was of the whiteness I'd been surrounded by, stuffed with, my entire life. I sought to replace it with an understanding of the people I belonged to but felt denied from, and the only way I felt I could do that was with the thing I've loved before I knew race. I found relief in an African American literature course.

Together, we read your *Sula*. I was struck by how honestly you wrote about humans. How you refused to shy away from our ugly, despair, our envy. You showed me how our past molds our very being—and that by ignoring it, we allow it to disfigure us. Your words weighed heavy on my mind and heart, but I welcomed that weight. My internal landscape crumbled under it, but through the cracks, something bright and magnificent was waiting. It was through your crafted darkness that I learned what love could be. For the first time, I knew light, and I began to see it everywhere.

My professor planned to end the semester with *The Bluest Eye*, but finals crept up the way they always seem to despite the cyclical nature of schooling. I finished your first novel before Christmas.

Your stories changed my life. By putting the pieces of what. I struggled to accept together, you woke me up to what I've instinctively always known: There is no freedom, internally or globally, without truth. You showed me that nothing was ever wrong with me, that nothing is wrong with any of us, but we owe it to each other to try to be better. All within the span of three novels, a few interviews, a lecture, and a short story.

One more thing?

I'm newly broken each time I've finished one of your works. The trauma and pain you lay before me slip easily between the gaps of my memory.

But, somehow, my dreams are sweeter. You've woken a consciousness that is heavy, but in a way that makes me strong. I can imagine, almost touch, a world that is soft and kind. I wish you were still here so you could show me more, but I'm trying not to be greedy with what's yours.

Last thing, I promise.

I wonder what you saw when you wrote the place from which your character Beloved came. What Pecola looked like in your mind's eye.

If Twyla was the white one (because I'm willing to bet she is!). What it is you so dislike about *Sula* and how you'd change it.

Above all, I wonder if in some way, wherever you are, you'll read this. If you know it's more than respect or admiration I feel when I think of you. If you know just how vast the gap is that you've left us with. I hope you're close. I hope you know peace. I hope you know your work is prized and deeply cherished.

Thank you for teaching me that it is our duty to live up to our potential, and that it is possible. Thank you for setting the bar ridiculously high. Thank you for showing me that intelligence is useless without empathy. Thank you for demonstrating that there is strength in tenderness, and that I can hold some in my heart for every *other*. Thank you for tilling the soil; I hope my seeds are worthy of your garden.

I am eternally yours.

Love,
Pascale

Sylvia Plath

By Judah Berl

I have poisoned myself. I have hanged myself. I have murdered and murdered each of me that refuses, rejects perfection. I have asphyxiated myself just to write a poem.

It is a dangerous thing to hold sorrow so close, hug it like a mother. Today I told my own mother I love her, twice. I don't know how many years I have left with her. She poured the coffee, and we sat in the middle of the morning, watched our one fat squirrel ravage the bird feeder from the window. I love that squirrel, consuming without end, and I have consumed without end in my own life; I have begun to self-consume. I don't know how many years I have left.

Ninety-one years old today, you would've loved that squirrel too. I can see your gummy smile spread to your eyes as you watch him. Our one fat squirrel, unaware of his peanut-crunching crowd, yet performing nonetheless. Not us though. You and I—we can't sleep without a crowd these days. It is a dangerous thing to not sleep, and we do it well. We frenzy. We get into the car, drive until we turn onto a dead-end street, and we keep driving. I look at you in the passenger seat and you're not there; the last time you saw a squirrel was sixty years ago. And I keep driving.

To know you will die by your own hand is the heaviest thing. You carried it, I carry it; I can't help but wonder if I accidentally picked up yours. What is life supposed to do with those who reject it?

And then, like insatiable fat squirrels, we scurry to the bird feeder and shake with madness our only source of life. We gut the bird feeder. We steal the seed and eat it all at once. Overindulgence, after all, is perfectly sensible when you could die at any moment; you can die at any moment, and that thought keeps us. We create from pain and are lauded for it, and then we create pain in order to create. It is a dangerous thing.

After coffee, my mother and I go on a walk to keep things moving. As we make our way up the street, we see it: Not fifty feet from our driveway lay a road-killed squirrel, another fat one. Is this how they go? Glutting in birdseed just to throw themselves in front of a car? Is this how I will go? Do I envy a squirrel for knowing?

Or do I do my own indulgence in ignorance? I pretend fat squirrels are suicidal too. I pretend to be blind to the sad smiles of my mother, and when they catch onto my skin, I pretend to be paralyzed. My head is buried beneath the bird feeder today. It's all too much: the sorrow, the squirrels, the smiles, and the love of my mother. So I keep my head grounded, just like you, in the overwhelming hope that one day it won't be. One day I won't be.

But today I am. Today I'm thinking about you and squirrels. Dangerous, I know. Love can look like danger, and I hate the word "love" and I love the word "danger." I forgot to ask if I could love you. I forgot, for the life of me, to tell you the life you've given me. So I'll tell you one more thing about our squirrel.

He haunts me. I see him in my mind, standing finally at the foot of his fate. He is not patient, but he waits. Then, at once, he bounds across the expanse of asphalt, in time for the inevitable to drive its body into his. He is successful. He is successful the way you were successful. He is a scholar and a poet.

But today, I am not. Today I look at my mother beside me on our walk, and I latch a smile onto her skin too. It is not enough to keep me here. But it makes me wonder if I should let you and the squirrels live alone a little longer.

Mae West

By Kimberly J. Dalferes

I've been an avid thrifter for as long as I can remember. There were visits to five and dime stores with Nana in search of dented pans still capable of holding apple pies. I perused Goodwill stores to outfit myself in college, and it was thrilling to pull together an ensemble that cost less than a textbook. Today, I don't thrift out of necessity but for pure fun of the hunt. Thrifting is how I came upon Mae.

On a sunny morning, I wandered an outdoor market where vendors amassed aisles of secondhand finds and one-of-a-kind treasures. I lingered over stacks of colorful blankets, wondered at the patina of well-worn wooden kitchen spoons, and picked through boxes of tarnished keys. As I turned an aisle corner, I noticed a booth with a large table at its center, strewn with stacks of photos.

These 8 x 10 black-and-white glossies appeared to be Hollywood publicity photos from the 1930s. Tucked in the stacks was a snapshot of a starlet posing at a desk, a wide-brimmed hat askew atop her blonde curls. A jacket sporting a white applique over the shoulder somewhat obscures the plunging neckline of her dress. Scripted in the photo's margins is her name: Mae West. I took Mae home with me, where she came to rest in a frame on my desk.

I began researching Mae and was amazed by her background. Born in Brooklyn in 1893 to a corset-modeling mother and jack-of-all-trades father (including but not limited to bare-knuckles boxing), she began her career as a teenage vaudevillian under the stage name Baby Mae. By all accounts she loved the spotlight and the wild unpredictability of theater life. It's Mae who's often credited with starting the sexy shimmy dance craze of the 1920s, taking Black culture to White audiences via her stage performances.

I was surprised to learn she was a prolific playwright. Mae's plays were raw reflections of women who refused to be controlled by those in power. Her Broadway play *Sex* landed her in jail for violating obscenity laws. She relished the publicity and spoke of not minding jail one bit, except for the burlap underwear, which she replaced with her own silk undies.

Mae's rise in Hollywood was meteoritic—and plagued the Puritan censors who worked around the clock to tame her. This was the celluloid temptress most of us envision: hand on the hip of a lavish gown, dripping in jewels, wearing a tall hat and platform shoes to heighten her five-foot-tall frame, with her double entendres sneaking past the production code. Mae's naughty girl persona made her one of the highest paid actresses of the 1930s. Her 1933 film *She Done Him Wrong*, which she both wrote and starred in, had the second-highest gross, right behind *King Kong*. It's reported that by 1935, the only person with a higher paycheck than Mae was William Randolph Hearst. In an age of male dominance, she had full control of all aspects of her filmmaking—from writing to lighting to casting.

Gazing upon my treasured photo, I've wondered how Mae would answer the questions swirling in my thoughts.

Mae, do I drink too much?

I don't know, I never touched the stuff. I once discovered W. C. Fields drinking with the crew, and I had him thrown off set. Never happened again. Take a look in the mirror and decide for yourself. Don't matter what others think.

Mae, what's your take on gay marriage?

Marriage is a great institution, but I'm not ready for an institution yet. As for the homosexuals, I've always been their champion.

My play The Drag *was written for them. I'm thrilled for their right to marry if that's what they want.*

Mae, what do you think of today's actresses?

I think they're fabulous. They're smart, they know how to get ahead. They write, produce, and they use their fame to sell shampoo and clothes—it's divine. Very few women did that in my day—I was the only one.

Mae, am I too old to start a new career at 60?

Dearie, I was 60 when I started my Vegas show. I didn't even begin my film career until I was in my 40s. Remember, you only live once, but if you do it right, once is enough.

Mae left this world in 1980, but her image and words endure. May we all be so lucky.

Though I do believe Mae would say luck had nothing to do with it.

Lily Tomlin

By Julie Danis

The first time I laughed out loud during the 1985 Broadway production of *The Search for Signs of Intelligent Life in the Universe* happened when Chrissy, one of the many characters inhabited by Lily Tomlin, says, "All my life I've always wanted to *be* somebody. But I see now I should have been more specific."

Me too, Lily. I'm glad I'm not the only one.

How do people figure out what they want to *be* when they grow up? When I was in preschool, I was often asked:

Julie, what do you want to be when you grow up?

I would answer:

I want to be happy.

Now, happy is sweet, but it's not very actionable.

This one-woman show written by Lily Tomlin's partner, Jane Wagner, follows Trudy, a bag lady and former creative consultant to Nabisco, as she gives aliens a tour of the planet. She tells Nabisco, "You could be the first to sell the concept of munching to the Third World. We got an untapped market here! These countries got millions and millions of people who don't even know where their next *meal is coming* from. So the idea of eatin' *between* meals is somethin' just never occurred to 'em!"

This time I laughed so hard, I snorted. At the time I was an Assistant Product Manager at Frito-Lay, attempting to create a market for a morning snack called Fruit Pastrie. A pointless task. No one wanted a triangular, two-bite Pop-Tart with less ersatz fruit filling.

As a girl, I dreamed of being an actress. In high school I was part of a half-hour television series—a squeaky-clean teenage version of *Rowan & Martin's Laugh-In*. Lily's characters on the network show, Ernestine

110

and Edith Ann, grabbed me. They showed me I didn't need to be goofy like Goldie Hawn, take a pie in the face like Judy Carne, or be loud like Jo Anne Worley to get a laugh. Smarts and sass work too. While neither Ernestine nor Edith Ann prepared me for a theater career or even success in acting class, they and other Lily characters from *Saturday Night Live* and movies kept me entertained and inspired as I went from theater major to social worker to consumer marketer and beyond.

A few years after encountering Lily's truth-talking Trudy, I left Frito-Lay and returned to my adopted hometown, Chicago. I went from fussing over fried pork rinds to conducting research on toilet paper habits and searching for a creative outlet to answer the siren song of the stage. The Second City's improvisation training program did just that.

Lily's influence appeared in the characters I performed. A precocious cookie-selling Girl Scout outsmarting her adult customers. A supercilious librarian lamenting the lack of family values in fairy tales. A facilitator in a Vocations Anonymous group who can't make it past Step One in the *7 Steps to Success*—each one expressing an irony or point of view in a way people would listen.

My favorite persona was a version of myself, the modern working woman trying to have it all. Channeling my inner-Lily, I spoke the truth of my experience and offered commentary on paradoxes found in white-collar work. I became a workplace humorist and wrote a newspaper column for the *Chicago Tribune* while still holding down a benefit-paying job. When my column was dropped, I was left without an outlet to express my work life observations except in the office. No one laughed.

Late in my marketing career, I taught marketers how to write brand purpose statements. Yes, an Oreo does have a purpose beyond satisfying a sweet tooth. One student's evaluation struck me: "She's funny." That made my day, and while I considered that a compliment, my manager didn't. So I decided to start looking for my purpose. I retired and began reinventing myself. As what, I wasn't sure, but I knew writing and humor would play a part.

At the same time, *Grace and Frankie* entered my living room. "Amen," I said. It was obvious. I've always wanted to be Lily Tomlin. Like her, I want to speak my truth and make people laugh in shared recognition of an experience. I want to make people feel heard and hugged, like Lily made me feel when I saw her on Broadway. I have written a one-woman show about my reinvention. It's a coming of middle-age story, which might not have an ending. But that's okay. As Lily Tomlin said, "The road to success is always under construction."

Flo Kennedy

By Ebony Murphy

I often ponder the lives of women who lived before me in much harsher circumstances than I have had to endure. I hold in utmost regard women who thrived under virulent sexism, soared above open racism, attained impressive levels of education, made art when they could have made excuses, and crafted beautiful lives even and especially when money was short. Florynce Rae Kennedy, she of the quick wit, jaunty hats, political buttons, and a gold whistle she wore to "blow the whistle on the man," is one of these women.

Flo Kennedy graduated from Columbia Law School in 1951. She earned her undergraduate degree three years earlier, in 1948, working her way through and finishing in her early 30s. A Black woman with two Ivy League degrees who made her way from Kansas City, Missouri, to Harlem before the Civil Rights Act and the Voting Rights Act? I haven't yet constructed the perfect Flo Kennedy Halloween costume, but I am working on it.

In the 2011 documentary *Gloria: In Her Own Words*, Flo is shown at the 1972 DNC berating the media for their sensationalist coverage of the feminist movement while declining to interview Shirley Chisholm and her supporters. Flo was also a skilled fundraiser and organizer, helping to keep *Ms. Magazine*, the National Organization for Women, the Feminist Party, and National Black Feminist Organization afloat. She knew that activism required not just bravery and a big mouth but also resources and money. To get those things you needed to be able to look folks in the eyes and not shirk away. She coauthored a book called *Abortion Rap* after her work on the *Abramowicz v. Lefkowitz* case that predated *Roe v. Wade*. Of her parents, who raised five girls, she said, "My parents gave us a fantastic sense of security and worth: By the time the bigots got around to telling us that we were nobody, we already knew we were somebody."

In 1974 *People* magazine labeled Flo "the biggest, loudest and indisputably, the rudest mouth on the battleground where feminist activists and radical politics join in mostly common cause." Flo was thrilled. Historian Sheri M. Randolph, who wrote *The Life of a Black Feminist Radical*, described Flo as "stridently Black." Women like me and like Flo—dark-skinned, unambiguously Black with hair like Esther Rolle—are easy to demonize and stereotype. Our anger, when it cannot be used in the service of others, is often used to caricature us and deny us professional opportunities, social equality, and even decent medical care. Flo knew all this and didn't let it silence her. She titled her 1976 memoir *My Hard Life and Good Times*, and she saw all the movements of her day as connected. She debated Betty Friedan and Billie Holiday and berated Senator Daniel Patrick Moynihan as a "racist sexist bastard." Flo knew how to have a good time. Anyone from Bella Abzug to H. Rap Brown was liable to show up in her Rolodex and at her birthday gatherings and parties.

Flo died in 2000, the same year I graduated high school. Like Flo, who was outrageous and fun, and collected friends from corners of the city and county, I try my best not to let the heavy issues of the day steal my joy. Though she didn't live to see Kimberlé Williams Crenshaw's term "intersectionality" become mainstream, Flo's life and work showcased that very notion.

I am not L, G, B, or T, but I am Q if I use bell hooks' definitions: "'Queer' not as being about who you're having sex with (that can be a dimension of it); but 'queer' as being about the self that is at odds with everything around it and that has to invent and create and find a place to speak and to thrive and to live." As a 41-year-old woman who chooses not to be a mother and as a secondary teacher of fifteen years now, my life is unlike that of my mother and her mother, who both married early, navigated breast cancer, and died young. Along with their memories, I need other women whose paths were unorthodox and nontraditional to guide me.

Flo believed, "Powerlessness is a dirty word." I believe that too. Sometimes you can't wait until the world is ready for you to be free.

You must live as if you already are free and see what happens.

Virginia Woolf

By Margaret E. Mitchell

"Mrs. Dalloway said ..."

I scan the flowers in the grocery store: cheap, cheerful bouquets past their prime. Mrs. Dalloway would turn her nose up at them.

"... she would buy the flowers herself." Well, who else would buy them? I laugh and select a bunch that still has buds and no luridly dyed carnations. (Mrs. Dalloway averts her eyes politely.)

That is one version of fame: to have written sentences so memorable that they take up residence in the minds of strangers a century later, getting trotted out at the grocery store by people to whom characters you dreamed up and committed to paper are as real as if they had lived.

In her *Writer's Diary*, Woolf recounts walking through St. James's Square while in the midst of rereading *Moll Flanders* and seeing people—"a woman selling matches," a "draggled girl"—through the eyes of Daniel Defoe. "Yes, a great writer surely," she muses, "to be there imposing himself on me after two hundred years." She worries that she does not possess that power; critics have complained that she has not yet created "characters that survive." But if Mrs. Dalloway is with me at Publix, then she must have, after all; now she is the one doing the imposing.

She would like that, I think.

The *Diary* reveals that Woolf had a vexed relationship with fame. She longed for it and feared it; she basked in it and retreated from it. "The psychology of fame is worth considering at leisure," she writes during a period when she has been especially inundated with praise, and often in the *Diary* she does just that. At one moment she concedes that someone's praise has given her "immense pleasure"; at another she wonders why a word of criticism has so much more power than any amount of praise; at another she insists that she takes neither praise nor blame "excessively to heart." We know better than to believe her—there is too much evidence in the *Diary* to the contrary—but we let it slide, because the *Diary* is a conversation with herself. And when she's talking to herself, she so frequently contradicts herself on the subject of fame that it humanizes her; she becomes not Woolf the Important Author but an anxious writer hoping to be liked, wondering what success means.

Woolf's greatest fear about fame was that it would interfere with writing. By the time each novel came out, she was always at work on the next, intent upon finding some new narrative form to give shape to a new idea. She worried that she might become reliant on adulation: "Unpraised, I find it hard to start writing in the morning." But she reassured herself that after working for half an hour, she always remembered why she wrote: not for praise but for her "pleasure in the art." For the *Diary* is, above all else, a chronicle of work. Of labor. She kept a strict writing schedule: so many words before tea; so many pages a week; so many weeks for a novel.

Two years ago, I rented a tiny cabin in north Georgia for a week to revise a novel. I brought nothing to read but the books I needed for research and Woolf's *Writer's Diary.*

One night in the cabin, I awoke and saw a bright round light drifting around the room, dancing along the ceiling. I watched it for a moment with pure pleasure: It was a rotund little fairy, a messenger from another dimension. It was magical. And then I reached out for my glasses and the fairy resolved itself into a lightning bug.

In the morning I recorded the experience in my diary, and it occurred to me that if I were Virginia Woolf, I would spin it into a dazzling metaphor—for language, for life, for happiness, for something.

Instead, I sat down at the kitchen table and opened my laptop. We cannot be Virginia Woolf; our sentences will never cut like perfect diamonds, and we do not need to grapple with our fame as we settle down to write. It doesn't matter. What matters, Woolf knew, is the settling down. The words on the page, one after another after another. The work. There's no point in having a room of your own if you use it to scroll through social media and dream of the novels you could write if only, if only. What matters, Woolf reminds us, is the work.

Gertrude Stein

By Sydney Melocowsky

Before Stein, I never asked an object for its pronouns. I never inquired about what a blue plate observed or if it collected hobbies rather than dust while atop the kitchen shelf. I gave fabrics names out of convenience rather than identity. But fabric—texture—is perhaps only a delineated, sensory experience which people anthropomorphize.

By calling it "fabric," I have already engaged in the process of identifying its value; its usefulness is determined by its relationship to me. Fabric is wearable, and what is wearable is inferior to me. A human does not wear the skin of another human except to exemplify his power; it is a process of oppression and erasure. To create fabric, I must first strip it. Its native tongue must be cut so it cannot speak its own language. I give the object a new name. Now the tongue says, "Made in China" or "Made in Bangladesh," but its making was before the factory. I give the object a name it does not understand. Disorienting the object makes it more human.

Humans only know how to succeed through subjugation. The fabric does not need to know itself—only I do. I need to be able to identify it with ease. The fabric must be unaccented and compartmentalized as an entity of application.

I enslave the object to make it human. My shirt becomes a shirt in places I can't see, through the palms of embalmed entities who rattle rather than speak. These entities are machines. They are man-made, sometimes handmade, sometimes made by the hands of bigger machines. Is *making* preservation or destruction?

It is a privilege to stand in the corner of a room, exclaim that I am in the center, and to have an audience of peers agree with me. The human perspective is ego-centered. Each one of us believes to be the sun in his own, solipsistic solar system of existence. Inside the room I inhabit, the walls are worlds around me in a nearly constant state of winter. I see them according to my own position: Their lives face away from my own and exist to me as a point of contrast. They are walls. I am sentient. Their summer exists only as long as I offer my own emotions to them; they may express themselves solely in relation to me. They are walls while I eat breakfast. They become obscure when I leave the room.

Before Stein, multifacetedness was reserved for people. I believed myself to be the most enigmatic mosaic of fragments, scattered across the people I'd touched and the places I'd been. I ordained myself divine from the god within me and decided myself omniscient; that which I didn't know ceased to matter. I threaded the fabric of man, sacred specs of stolen ethereality, on a loom of a singular lifeline. Humanity glowed golden and bled shades of sensuality I could only believe made us incarnate, made us real. I saw the fabric as a single, self-made thing.

Before Stein, I never construed humanity as a projection of the universe's borrowed parts. Of roasts. Of tender buttons. Of roses. And roses. And roses. My memories are not my own. My brain is but a vessel to hold and serve memories on behalf of placated, porcelain party guests. My life is composed of moments and those moments composed of pictures. Of objects. Of things that collect and preserve. That fear and scream. That console and indulge. They are silent themselves but storied; they allow my own interpretations to silence me. I carry these things as splinters of perspective, vestiges lost in the folds of human skin.

Everything is, and is composed of, fabrics—worn and torn and left as semblances of something more. The clatter of Tupperware calculating its tumble is muffled by the cupboard. The oak cabinets make for decent acoustics inside. There is a concert in my kitchen. A funeral under the floorboards. Under the sole of someone's shoe is the soul of an unsuspecting vagrant. There is a massacre at the dinner table. Stale bread decays in crumbs on a white sheet. The cloth conceals the shrapnel of rice grains scattered across the stagnant plane. The stem of a wine glass surveys the surviving scene and scans for other salvageable scraps. It notices glints of glass and the remnants of something that once had a lip. It recognizes the rim and stares into the spilled Burgundy drying into the contrasting cloth.

While the adjacent room is at war, I am in bed. Asleep.

Edith Wharton

By Emily Parrow

I learned that American novelist Edith Wharton nearly set part of *The Age of Innocence* in the Blue Ridge Mountains, and that small detail brought me to her doorstep.

Picture me on my knees in an unfamiliar Massachusetts apartment, slotting books onto the gaping shelves of a stark, black bookcase. Just hours ago, my mother's voice broke over my shoulder in yet another farewell, and I am startled to realize I have said goodbye to at least one person I love every single day this week.

To settle myself—and distract myself from the settling—I have decided to unpack my books.

The Custom of the Country, The House of Mirth, Summer.

Wharton felt more herself in the Berkshires than she ever did in fashionable New York and Newport. As a twentysomething with imposter syndrome, I'm covetous of her resolve. I long for the same conviction that I am destined to thrive in a specific place.

And because I've carried the old bruise of my own family's uprooting from New England for nearly a decade, I long believed it was here in the Northeast that I belonged.

My parents brought me to the Blue Ridge Mountains' doorstep the summer I turned 16—an age ripe for taking the move, and everything else, personally. We left our Connecticut farm at six in the morning, the fog blurring the scene like condensation on a bathroom mirror.

Since we were babies, my sisters and I had taken for granted going free-range over our Connecticut stone wall–edged kingdom. Sunflowers bent their faces over marvelous flower gardens and stood sentry with the pear trees and wild blackberry bushes. The barn, built in 1939 as a post-hurricane construction, was regal and red.

The night before our southbound departure, my sisters and I walked through every naked room of the farmhouse, the rugs rolled up at our feet, and reminisced like old women.

Six months later, at a high school from which I furiously wished to be unenrolled, my English teacher assigned *Ethan Frome*. She gifted me my first glance into what Wharton called in another novel, "Custom of the Country," called "hieroglyphic world."[1] Reading her words, I felt as if I came into an inheritance.

I thumb the same annotated copy of *Ethan Frome* now. That little spine was a fraying tether to nine years in a place I swore I'd one day leave—and happily.

Setting *Ethan* aside, I peel open a box of books about Gilded Age America—the spoils of my history degree. Evelyn Nesbit's memoir fits between histories of Newport lighthouses, Progressive Era housing reform, and the debutante ritual.

My phone illuminates with an unanswered text from my best friend. We met my third semester of college at a place that nurtured bashful spring shoots of belonging in that new Virginia clay, where my studies revealed the devastating significance of Wharton's yellow roses and opera boxes like invisible ink.

Did you make it??

Her text makes me wistful for our summers together. We'd bake in the sun with library books and end the days with breakfast for dinner. We found ample things to love about that little college town, our hard-won brief home: walking trails over the river, flowering trees at the start of a long spring, November colors, and thrift stores full of knickknacks and secondhand furniture with which I decorated my first apartment.

I picture myself in that space just days ago, waddling across the bare floor, hands hooked under the weight of scavenged moving boxes. Three college students had carried off my couch, and the room was starting to echo. A thumbprint of spackle pockmarked the lonely expanse of green-gray wall, now void of its picture frames. Tearless grief caught in my throat each time I looked at it.

I left Virginia at six in the morning, the sunrise pink along the mountains' backbone.

Feeling strange to be back in the Northeast, where the accent rings familiar but the town names are brand-new, I'm skittish as a deer. Uprooted all over again. Wharton called the Berkshires her "first real home." I wonder if it will be mine.[2]

The patchwork of my bookshelf is assembled, and it's golden hour. A breeze hisses through the waist-high hayfields outside. Impossible to pass up a walk at this time of day. On my way out the door, I text my friend back, tell her I miss her, and hope she knows how much.

I stroll down a sloping gravel road with new mountains vast around me, and I name the flowers I encounter like I'm greeting old friends.

Coneflower, black-eyed Susan, Queen Anne's lace.

In my head like incantations, these flowers call to me from my mother's garden. Wharton calls to me from her books on my shelf, from the rooms of her home, The Mount, where I now have the good grace to be able to work, to read, to write.

Joy Ladin

Trace Peterson

Joy Ladin has just handed in her poetry thesis to the MFA program at UMass Amherst. She is taking a walk outside, after many frustrating workshops in which her "performances were not really valued that much." Ladin has also known since five years old—when she also first knew she was a poet—that she is a transgender woman. But on this spring evening in 1995, she has not transitioned yet and is unable to "imagine what ... the voice I would have if I lived as a woman, might be."

Ladin walks outside pondering the difficulty of being understood by others in the workshop. She thinks how "futile" it seems, how "sick" she is of the way she is writing. And she "hears a voice" that says:

"Well, why don't you write like someone else then?"

"Like who?" Ladin responds derisively.

"Anna Ascher," says the voice,

And suddenly a person's biography appears in Ladin's mind: "a Czech-German Jewish poet who ... was the daughter of a concert pianist, had spent her adolescence in a concentration camp, and was now living in 1950s Prague." Ladin goes home and writes the name and biography "at the top of a clean notebook page."

The next day she woke up and began writing "words that weren't mine, a series of short, allusively violent poems that appeared as though of their own accord." Because the voice said Anna was "'someone else,' someone who was nothing like me," Ladin adopted the strategy that "whenever I got stuck, I just wrote something that I, as myself, would never say." Somehow "for the first time," the trans but pre-transition Ladin felt "I was writing in the voice of a woman." For five years she channeled the voice of Anna, who seemed to have her own life independent of Ladin.

In the resulting text, Anna writes in her diary, "My muse is rage not beauty." Ladin notes, "My muse ... the muse inspiring my attempt to transform gender from a mode of repression into a mode of creation— was Anna." Poets since Homer have said. "Sing in me, muse" when composing, but this was new. By speaking in the voice of her muse but maintaining the reality of that voice and imagining Anna in turn as a writer who also has a muse, Ladin created a Möbius strip, or *mise en abyme*. She placed herself in a position of writerly agency, in between subject positions, that would be a space to temporarily "inhabit a form of female subjectivity." From this position she could speak powerfully about both Anna's Holocaust suffering and Ladin's own trans pain.

The Book of Anna is first published by Sheep Meadow Press in 2006 as Ladin's second book. Ladin still wants to transition, and her wife— who is unsupportive of transness—loves the book and has encouraged its writing. During the decade since she first heard the voice, Ladin has completed a PhD program at Princeton, started a family, and begun a job as professor at Yeshiva University. The book comes out authored by "J Ladin" without pronouns in the bio, signifying, if only to Ladin herself, her changing gender. So this innovative text which should rightfully be famous, a book central to trans literature, gets published without any blurbs, is not promoted by the publisher, and quickly disappears. The next year, after getting tenure at Yeshiva, Ladin is now finally able to transition and becomes herself—at a tremendous cost, but that is another story for another time.

And what does this story have to do with me? I saw, as Joy's friend, the brilliance of this out-of-print book in 2019, when concentration camps returned to the news. As a trans woman, I too understood how difficult telling our stories becomes in retrospect, when pressured by the dramas, the obstacles, the hate that the world keeps throwing in our paths; how difficult it is to match our external circumstances with our inner potential and be read—as who we wish to be and really are.

Dear Reader, I republished the book. Under Joy's real name this time. And we did new publicity and framed it right. And this time it won the National Jewish Book Award.

Zora Neale Hurston

By Rachel Pienta

I gripped my coffee cup with two hands, savoring that first hit of caffeine. In a few weeks I would be set free. I had big plans. Dawn was breaking along the coast of the Gulf of Mexico, but the beach and sparking sands weren't part of my summer dreams. For one glorious week I would get to immerse myself in the amazing, controversial life and works of Zora Neale Hurston in Eatonville, Florida. I taught a unit on the novel *Their Eyes Were Watching God* every year in my Advanced Placement Literature classes. A novel written by a famous Floridian, about places that youth might know, with a hurricane playing a major role in the narrative—the book was perfect for teaching critical analysis to Florida teens. With my Women's Studies students at the university, my approach to studying Hurston was as much about her controversial life as it was about her works.

It was almost time for me to head to my classroom at the local high school. It was the middle of May, the homestretch of the school year for Floridian teachers and students. By June, teachers and students are set free. Students were thinking about finals and graduation. I was thinking about my summer plans and my reading list to prepare for the university evening classes I would teach in the fall. The real jewel of my summer plans was the much-anticipated National Endowment of the Humanities grant-funded residency.

Hurston famously lied about her age to qualify for a free high school education; she was in her late 20s but passed for high school age. After receiving that hard-earned high school diploma from the state of Maryland, she graduated from Howard University. She began but never finished her doctorate at Columbia.

From her birth in the 1890s to her death in 1960, Hurston lived a life that defied the rules of her time. She traveled, wrote acclaimed works, and pushed the limits of social boundaries for women of the era. When she hit hard times, she worked as a maid so she could continue to write. A Black woman who came of age in the Jim Crow era, she studied the experience of her people and ancestors as an anthropologist and wrote multiple works that have endured and continue to serve as foundational canon.

The message alert on my cell phone beeped, disturbing my coffee daydreams about the coming summer. *A text at this hour?* I grabbed my phone from the kitchen table. My sister Sara had sent me a terse message, "Don't say you told me so; I am at the hospital. They found a mass."

I hit speed dial and Sara's voice filled my kitchen. "I finally went to the hospital. They are saying it is my liver, an advanced stage of cancer."

My brain began to race, words tumbling quickly from my lips. "We need a second opinion, we'll fight this together, I will be there tonight, I will leave right after school."

I wanted to believe that the cancer cannot be as bad as it sounds. My sister, like Zora Neale Hurston, had lived an unconventional life. She had gone from exotic dancing in Orlando nightclubs to being a social worker helping women and children move from domestic violence into safe spaces.

Sara was 31 that summer. A young mother with a toddler, her life was just beginning. The hours at school pass in a blur. By evening I was standing at my sister's bedside in an Ocala hospital, not far from Hurston's Eatonville.

A new course for the summer is plotted. I went from summer Hurston scholar to family caretaker, spending the school break caring for my nephew and sister with my parents on the family farm in Bushnell. I lived sixty miles from Eatonville that summer, but a world and years away from the summer of my May daydreams.

That summer ended with a hurricane. Tropical storm Fay battered Florida with four historic landfalls in the final week of August. When the winds subsided and the rains were gone, so was my sister. Back in my classroom after summer's end, I thought of Hurston's characters Janie and Teacake waiting for the hurricane in the darkness, while their eyes were watching God.

Helen Keller

By Mary Klages

I teach an undergraduate course at the University of Colorado at Boulder called Introduction to Disability Studies. This year I asked the students to make a list of the famous people they know who have disabilities. The name "Helen Keller" did not appear on their lists. Their top pick was Stephen Hawking.

I was surprised. Why didn't my students know about Helen Keller? After all, she had been one of the most famous representatives of disability in the twentieth century.

Keller was a media star beginning at age 8, in 1888, when newspapers picked up on the success of her education at the Perkins School for the Blind. She was portrayed as a child prodigy, and as a living representative of the human spirit's ability to overcome all obstacles. Newspapers around the country, and eventually around the world, reported the stories of Helen's wonderful accomplishments, and helped present her as a phenomenon. She remained in the media spotlight all of her adult life.

Keller of course was acutely aware of her public persona, as was Annie Sullivan and all those who helped and advised Keller. Because her left eye looked odd, they made sure that photographs were always taken from an angle that obscured it, assuring that Keller looked like a pretty young woman. In 1911 Keller had her eyes enucleated and replaced with glass prosthetics, and in subsequent photographs both eyes gleam at the camera.

Keller and Sullivan appeared in the new medium of movies in 1919 with the filming of *Deliverance*, a mostly biographical story that showed Keller as a modern hero fighting for humanity. They appeared on the vaudeville stage for a few years, with audiences asking Keller questions and Sullivan interpreting for Keller's difficult-to-understand speech.

Keller became a spokesperson and fundraiser for the American Foundation for the Blind in 1924, a job she would hold for the rest of her life. This kept her in the public view, through her thousands of speeches and articles, but meant she had to mute her socialist politics.

Keller was everywhere in the twentieth century—in her publications, her public appearances, the newsreels that followed her around the world as the American ambassador for disability rights. A 1954 movie, *The Unconquered*, documented her global efforts on behalf of "the handicapped." By then she was enshrined as an American saint, which is why the production of *The Miracle Worker*, on television in 1957 and an Academy-award winning movie in 1962, was so shocking. The now-elderly woman, retired from public life, was portrayed as a wild child needing taming discipline to become human. *The Miracle Worker* told the "untold" story of Helen Keller. It made her famous for learning language at age 7, rather than for all the achievements of her adult life.

That wild child was the Helen Keller my students knew; the story has been retold countless times, in children's biographies and in television movies. It has also been critiqued countless times by Disability Rights activists who find Keller's saintly image constricting.

In *Blind Rage: Letters to Helen Keller* (2006), for example, Georgina Kleege expresses resentment toward Keller, who was held up to the blind girl as a role model. In my course, we discussed Keller and *The Miracle Worker* under the heading "Inspiration Porn." I ask my students to write a question or comment at the end of each class session. After our discussions about Helen Keller, here's what appeared:

"Learning about Helen Keller was fascinating to me. I couldn't help but think about how much more incredible her contributions to the world could've been with modern-day technology."

My students wanted Helen Keller to be more like Stephen Hawking—someone who could overcome disabilities not through the triumph of the human spirit, but through assistive technologies.

They were not surprised when we found a new version of Keller's story that did exactly that.

Helen Killer is the title of four issues of a graphic narrative that posits Alexander Graham Bell making a device called an "Omnicle," which focuses light and sound waves into Keller's brain and enables her to see and hear. This unleashes a being Keller calls "Phantom"—which was the real Keller's name for herself before the acquisition of language. "Phantom" in the story is full of rage. She discovers that Bell's technology also gives her the ability to detect evil, so she becomes a superhero avenging wrongdoing by releasing the violence of her rage against evildoers—including those who would endanger people with disabilities.

Helen Keller lives on for the twenty-first century.

Simone de Beauvoir

By Emily Heiden

When I open my yellowed copy of *The Second Sex*, it falls immediately to the introduction, where see a passage I underlined when I was 15:

> If woman seems to be the inessential that never becomes the essential, it is because she herself fails to bring about this change ... women lack concrete means for organizing themselves into a unit ... they live dispersed among the males, attached through residence, housework, economic condition, and social standing to certain men—fathers or husbands—more firmly than they are to other women.

Who can say why I underlined that passage? Maybe I understood just enough to predict what was coming. I'd been reading de Beauvoir as a teenager because there were certain things at church and school that bothered me. I wanted a framework to help me understand the hazy injustices I perceived.

De Beauvoir turned out not to be the writer to provide that framework at 15—I gave up after the intro—but upon reopening the text, now at the age of 40, I feel called out by its lines, which underscore women's complicity in our own lack of freedom.

I've done some things to bring about change and entered the battle to fight the injustices that society heaps upon women. On National Public Radio I told the story of how I got duped by a fake pregnancy clinic, educating listeners about what really goes on in these centers. I've published about my abortion in books and online journals and told my own story.

But there are also ways in which I have failed to bring about change. For example, I went against my deepest instincts and changed my name when I got married. I did so because I teach, and my students were googling me and finding my writing about abortion. I didn't want to alienate those in my classroom who held different beliefs. And to be honest, the higher-ups at work expressed concern about my writing. Also, a group of my male students somehow called my cell phone at midnight on a Saturday. An anonymous student wrote: "You're not pro-choice, you're anti-life" on a whiteboard in my classroom.

This all happened during the year I taught under my maiden name. Now that name is fading into history, as is my sense of my single self. My guilt, however, is rising. Am I acting out of a lack of courage? Have I made decisions to keep myself from dealing with matters that, seventy-five years after the publication of *The Second Sex*, still define women's lives?

I feel that guilt spill over in my classroom. I recently overheard one of my students saying to her friend, "I love my last name. But then I remember one day I'll have to change it. And that's tough. I'm a first-name, last-name person."

"You don't *have* to change your name, Katie," I interjected.

"I know ... ," she said. "But I think I want to. I'm just sad."

I felt impotent and ridiculous. I wanted to look at her and say, "Hey, I didn't change mine."

But I did.

I wanted badly to be a changemaker and use my own life as a conduit, to be an example. But in this essential form of identity, I allowed myself to be subsumed.

I do mean it when I say subsumed. An envelope arrived in the mail last week addressed to Mr. and Mrs. My Husband's First and Last Name. Something in me screamed when I saw it. I want a world in which it would not seem unimaginable that a woman's first and last name might collectively stand for a couple.

De Beauvoir herself struggled with the feeling of being erased. She was not taken seriously by her male contemporaries; too often seen as simply having adopted the ideas of her lifelong partner, Jean-Paul Sartre, rather than being credited as a shaping force in his ideas—or having ideas of her own. The men around her didn't have much interest in her work, which dealt with women's inner lives. So she decided to articulate why her ideas mattered in an incredibly ambitious book—which of course became the seminal work we now know as *The Second Sex*. The book is credited with ushering in second-wave feminism. It's time to reintroduce its essential ideas to the next generation while reminding ourselves of their importance—and recognizing what still needs to be done to establish and maintain a woman's standing in the world.

Margaret Mead

By Sarah Strauss

"Are you there, Margaret? It's me, Sarah."

My name is Sarah and I'm an anthropologist. Fifty years ago, being a woman and an anthropologist meant only one thing: Margaret Mead. Among the most influential public intellectuals of the twentieth century, Margaret is now remembered by few beyond Anthropologyland.

In 2012, while working on a major federal grant proposal about the scintillating (but important) topic of the Rocky Mountain pine bark beetle epidemic—an impact of climate change that also provided a potential source of biofuel—one of the last steps was listing names of collaborating researchers. One was a soil scientist, another an economist; others were ecologists or sociologists, but the two anthropologists were identified as "social scientists." When I asked the principal investigator why not "anthropologists," he said, "But, Sarah! If we identified you that way, the federal reviewers would ask, why is Margaret Mead listed on this proposal? What does she have to do with beetle kill and biofuels in the American West?" We replied that Margaret Mead was exactly the kind of scientist this project needed, given the federal requirement to show how this research was relevant for American society. And so Mead's disciplinary descendant, "Sarah Strauss, Anthropologist," was listed as a co-investigator for that successful $10 million USDA grant.

The project leader was not wrong to think that a public intellectual best known for work on sexuality, gender, and child development on tropical islands might have little to say about the human dimensions of climate change. But in 1975, as the second female (and still the only female social scientist) president of AAAS (publishers of *Science* magazine), Margaret convened a conference titled "The Atmosphere: Endangered and Endangering"; the participants were a veritable who's who of climate science royalty, including Wally Broecker, James Lovelock (of Gaia hypothesis fame), presidential advisor John Holdren, and Stephen Schneider. Mead was also one of the earliest contributors to the emergent 1950s field of "Cybernetics" that later became known as Computer Science/Artificial Intelligence.

The midcentury discussions that occurred on these "hard" science themes included perspectives derived from our diverse sociocultural wisdom and practice because of Mead's wide-ranging intellect and ready grasp of humanity's need to engage in equally hard conversations about how to imagine a better future for us all. Winthrop Sargeant's 1961 *New Yorker* portrait ("It's all anthropology!") highlighted this broad sweep of Mead's gaze: Anything to do with people, their languages, cultures, histories, bodies, and imaginations is fit for anthropological study, and we all benefit from such explorations. This is what I teach my students today.

Margaret's PhD dissertation, published as *Coming of Age in Samoa* (1928), catapulted the 27-year-old to fame; this study of the "Flappers of the South Seas" suggested that nurture, not nature, determined stormy American adolescence. The book launched a storied career, framing sexuality as culturally defined and questioning contemporary assumptions on multiple themes. Mead's popular public persona was seen very differently by many academics; she was the subject of massive controversy, and some claims about the variable quality of her many writings did have merit. Yet her influence and her insistence on the relevance of anthropological research for the everyday lives of individuals, and the critical power of local communities to take their own futures in hand, cannot be overestimated.

Margaret warned younger scholars of the academic dangers that writing for popular audiences could bring; as a graduate student, I experienced a taste of this. A visa issue disallowed my continuing work in another Indian community where I had conducted preliminary research, so I switched my PhD topic to contemporary yoga practice in Rishikesh—a subject that had, surprisingly, received little academic attention. A faculty advisor invoked Mead without naming her, saying that this decision meant I would forever be known as the "Yoga Lady," never to escape early work on such a popular topic.

Although yoga continues to inform my academic endeavors, I, like Margaret, went on to explore many other topics of contemporary interest, from herbal medicine to beetle-killed forests; from the social life of water to the importance of community climate adaptation, where her most famous quote—"Never doubt that a small group of thoughtful committed citizens can change the world; indeed, it is the only thing that ever has"—continues to motivate me to become even a faint image of the public luminary that was Margaret Mead.

Thank you, Margaret, for the courage and conviction you modeled for the rest of us, and for being the beacon, shadows and all, that illuminates the path forward.

Billie Jean King

By Aynsley Diamond

Billie Jean King is an advocate for equal pay in sports, an activist for LGBTQ2+ rights, and one of the most famous tennis players in the world. She used her fame to span barriers and give voice to inequalities in women's sport. Billie's most famous quote reads, "Unless I was number one, I wouldn't be listened to." Her concerns and ideas were powerful, yet she knew that unless she was the best, she did not have validity in the eyes of men.

Billie won thirty-nine Grand Slam titles between 1961 and 1979, with a number 1 ranking for six years. In 1972, after winning the women's singles title, she quietly stated, "I don't think we will be back if we don't have equal prize money." This obvious yet controversial statement set off a career in advocacy that spanned decades. The Women's Tennis Association was founded by King and eight other female tennis stars fifty years ago. The "Original 9" risked their careers and changed history when they banded together to create a women's professional tennis tour. All these years later, women are still fighting for fiscal equity in sports.

On my desk is a plaque that reads, "Underestimate me, that'll be fun." My career has been an exercise in watching the advancement of those with less drive, less education, less passion, but more penis. You've read the articles with advice for career advancement of women. They remind us that women undersell themselves and men oversell. That women need to reach back and help the progression of their sisters, that the glass ceiling can be breached by creating a diamond from coal, pressure, persistence, and time. What they don't tell you is you will be a bruised and bloody mess when you do succeed. And some of us lose a lot of ourselves along the way.

I imagine Billie looking across the net at Bobby Riggs thinking, *This shithead is who I have to beat to secure my legitimacy and help other women in the sport.* What she actually said was "To beat a 55-year-old guy was no thrill for me. The thrill was exposing a lot of new people to tennis."

I wish I had her poise. I wish that every time a male colleague is surprised by my intelligence, research, and drive that I did not visualize punching him in the throat. We all have the stories, the cringeworthy condescension, the belittling requests, the title of being an "angry woman." I am. Goddammit, I *am* mad. We believe that if we work just as hard as our male counterparts, our worth will be acknowledged. You aren't even offered a seat at the table unless, as Billie stated, you are "number one." The problem is that the table is moved across the court, toward my opponent, while the distance on my side of the net continues to grow. Many a brilliant woman has made the decision that the distance is just too far.

I must acknowledge the men who rail against typology. The men in my life are precious to me. My husband and son are two of the finest examples of humanity. I selectively surround myself with men who will fight for women and recognize their privilege.

My gender-nonconforming oldest child reminds me of the pleasures and pressures of gender in our society. They experience discrimination on a daily basis as they navigate their lifelong journey of finding who they want to be. I have it hard. They have it harder.

So where does that leave us, my friends? Love–love? According to tennisct.com, "In tennis, 'love' means zero. Scoring in tennis isn't like most other sports that follow a linear one, two, three type of progression.

When starting a game or a set, a rational person would think it's zero–zero. That would be true. But in tennis we say love–love."

My life has not followed a linear progression, nor do I feel like I am staring across the net with an equal and open score. Like many women, I am trying to balance being a success in my field, using my privilege to support those who have less, being a good wife, mother, friend, daughter, and sister. I carry this weight in addition to being told to "smile" and to "stay in your lane." The deck is still stacked against us on the sole basis of sex.

We navigate chauvinism daily—in the office, on the court, and in the boardroom. Inequity is a constant microaggression. I'll try to emulate Billie, her grace and composure, but I have worked too hard and given up too much not to celebrate my wins loudly. The point Bille taught me is the long game. The optics of showing the world how it's won, game by game, so that the collective statistics are undeniable. So keep smashing each shot; I'll be here in my power suit returning each stroke, focusing not on this game, or your ego, but on the future.

Jane Fonda

By Brenda Murphy

Jane Fonda likes to quote a critic's remark that her hair needed its own agent. It's certainly possible to trace her early career from the rather ditzy bleached blondes she played in early 1960s comedies like *Period of Adjustment* and *Barefoot in the Park*, characters who looked like Marilyn Monroe and dressed like Jackie Kennedy, to the shock that was *Barbarella* in 1968. This sci-fi send-up is all about sex. It begins with a zero-gravity striptease over the credits and goes on from there. Condemned by the Catholic Legion of Decency, *Barbarella* transformed Jane Fonda from newlywed next door to fantasy sex goddess. Although her costumes may seem tame by today's female superhero standards, to the eyes of 1968, Barbarella was all bare skin and Brigitte-Bardotesque blonde hair. But it was Jane Fonda who owned that image, that over-the-top, transgressive combination of sexiness and up-to-date fantasy space weapon.

In 1971 came *Klute* and the haircut. The no-nonsense character Bree Daniels with her long, straight shag got rid of the vestiges of Monroe and Bardot and occasioned Fonda's Oscar-winning performance as a cool, emotionally repressed call girl who aims to control every situation she's in. The haircut took on its own life in the 1970s. The anti–Vietnam War activist Jane Fonda is inseparable from the *Klute* haircut. For many, especially young women, it became the iconic image of a woman whose successful acting career took second place to her convictions. A woman who played in the arena with the men and did not back down.

Then in 1972 came the fateful mistake. During a tour of North Vietnam to publicize the threat that American bombing of the dike system posed to the civilian population, she was photographed sitting

143

on an antiaircraft gun surrounded by smiling North Vietnamese soldiers. This image immediately went viral and undermined her credibility with the general population. She became the infamous Hanoi Jane, a traitor to her country, the Tokyo Rose of the Vietnam War to its supporters. She has called this a "two-minute lapse of sanity that will haunt me forever" and has apologized numerous times for the pain it caused servicemen and their families. But for many, she will never, ever live it down.

In the traditional arc of a tragedy, this is the turning point, the moment when overweening pride leads to the heroine's downfall. Jane Fonda had never been more famous, but that fame had become infamy. Wherever she went, she faced protests, death threats, threats to her family. Fifty years later, they still surface. As she has said, "The photo exists, delivering its message regardless of what I was doing or feeling."

One of the extraordinary things about Jane Fonda is her ability to use the cultural capital of fame, ironically increased by infamy, to her own ends. After a few years, she revived her acting career by returning to her comic roots in *Fun with Dick and Jane*, the third-highest-grossing movie of 1977, and then built on her newly established power at the box office to make several films about issues that were important to her, most significantly, *Coming Home*, about returning Vietnam veterans, *The China Syndrome*, and *9 to 5*.

Then came *The Workout*. In 1982 Fonda released her *Workout Book* and accompanying VHS tape to support the Campaign for Economic Democracy, a political action committee she had started with her husband, Tom Hayden, to fund New Left causes. The series of books and tapes that became *The Workout* featured Fonda in her black tights and red and black–striped leotard, crowned with a long shag of soft natural blonde curls, a big, open smile on her face. It is largely credited with wresting the fitness movement from the likes of Jack LaLanne and setting off the workout craze that helped empower women in the 1980s. *The Workout* empire funded not only leftist causes but also Fonda's producing companies.

Fonda retired from the screen in 1991, took a decade out for Ted Turner, and in 2005 made another triumphant return via comedy, with the highly profitable *Monster-in-Law*. She has been back ever since, notably in her television series, *Grace and Frankie*, which highlighted many issues facing older Americans. At 85 she is still transforming the image of the feminine for a generation, out on the hustings advocating for climate change causes in a gray pixie cut that debuted with fanfare at the 2020 Oscars.

Susan B. Anthony

By Pammela Quinn

Me and Susan B.

My father never lost his childhood interest in coin collecting. When my sister and I were young, he would occasionally gift us coins and currency not in usual circulation: silver certificate dollars, half-dollar coins, $2 bills, etc. I kept them all in a Folgers coffee can I made into a piggy bank, mixed in with regular nickels, dimes, and quarters. The silver dollars were my favorite. I was completely fascinated that these coins were worth the same as the paper bills that paid for my school lunches. And that the small dollars—the Susan B. Anthonys—were somehow worth just as much, even though they could so easily be mistaken for a quarter!

In first grade I plotted to "fool" the lunch lady with a Susan B. The scene played out as I had hoped. When I handed her the coin, she told me it was not enough.

"It costs more than that!" she said.

"No, it doesn't," I contradicted. "That's a dollar, not a quarter!"

Her surprised look almost made it worth losing one of my special coins. Almost.

Not long after this, I realized that these "small" dollars were (at the time) the only money featuring a woman. Susan B.'s coin face provided my first conscious tip-off that women weren't viewed as equal political figures, a lesson I'd relearn more than once. But I knew that just as Susan B.'s size could fool people into thinking she was worth less than the manly Eisenhowers, her coins were equal in value all the same. They could surprise you.

My history classes continued to remind me that men were the main characters in public life. Women fuzzily existed only in the domestic sphere. My personal history paralleled this. I spent summers at my grandparents' place, my grandmother Alice in charge of all the homely tasks. Even in stories of my dad's childhood, Alice played the same domestic role—getting breakfast ready before her husband went off to his important job.

I was more surprised than the lunch lady when, the summer I turned 14, my grandmother casually mentioned something that happened when she "was in law school." Law school?! This little old lady in her apron had attended law school?! Why, yes, she had. In the 1930s. I sat with her on the couch and got to know her. It was like I was truly seeing her for the first time.

It turned out that Grandma Alice had been in the first class of women admitted to the University of Delaware. When she graduated in 1918, the handful of women in her class created a small yearbook appropriately called *The Pioneers*. (It has only recently reemerged from the university archives as an online PDF.) When I was leaving to study abroad in France, she surprised me again by offhandedly noting she had lived there too as a young woman. In her case, she had been a volunteer ambulance driver during WWI. During WWII, by then a law school graduate, she advocated for Japanese Americans and later became a founder of the Japan Society. I saw her large Japanese art collection, which I had grown up with and taken for granted, with sudden appreciation. It was not the hobby of a bored housewife but a facet of an accomplished professional.

Alice and Susan B. were both on my mind when I had my only (so far) opportunity to cast a ballot for a woman president. And I realized that even almost 30 years since her death at age 101, Alice can still surprise me. I was startled to realize when I did the math that Susan B.'s battle for the right to vote wasn't achieved until Alice was in her 20s. Alice had marched as a suffragette in her home state of Delaware—which failed to ratify the Susan B. Anthony Amendment (as it was then called)—just two years after she graduated from college. When the election of 2016 revealed that some still do not see women's true value, I thought of my grandmother not living to see a viable woman candidate for president. And Susan B. not living to see women go to the polls in 1920. And it makes me hopeful that the disappointments of the future may be things we do not yet see as real possibilities. I hope to be surprised.

Mary Ingraham
Bunting Smith

By Polly Ingraham

Hanging on the wall in my study is a framed cover of *Time*, dated November 3, 1961. It is a replica of an oil painting showing a woman with short gray hair and brown cat-eyeglasses facing a younger woman in a cap and gown, a tree in the background. The banner across the top left corner reads, "GIRLS IN COLLEGE: *They Have Scarcely Begun to Use Their Brains*." In the lower right corner, in a smallish font, we see "RADCLIFFE'S MARY BUNTING."

This woman, my father's older sister, was named president of one of the Seven Sisters in 1960, holding the position until 1972.

While my grandparents named her Mary, she soon became known by the nickname—don't ask me how this worked—Polly. My parents slogged through having four sons before having a daughter, and they decided I would be Polly from the get-go. In our extended family, she was Big and I, naturally, was Little.

Staying home from school for hunks of her youth because of various illnesses, including Spanish flu, she read voraciously. She and my father rode their ponies a lot. Only occasionally attending Quaker meeting with her mother, she set out to learn as much as she could about various religions, absorbing the entire Quran by age 12. She went on to earn a PhD in microbiology, got married and had four children, lived with her family in a basement while they built a house and tended goats, endured the death of her husband, became dean of Douglass College, was the first woman to be appointed to

149

the Atomic Energy Commission, and led Radcliffe during the years before it merged with Harvard. When she left the porch light on, it meant that students could drop in and talk to her.

Big Polly (after she remarried, her full name became Mary Ingraham Bunting Smith) isn't famous in a celebrity kind of way. In the world of higher education, though, she became widely admired. By the 1960s, many white middle-class women who could afford not to hold jobs were finishing college, but most were still becoming housewives, with no talk yet of work-life balance. Soon after she began her new position in Cambridge, she launched the Radcliffe Institute for Independent Study, providing fellowships to women who needed more time and space to finish something they had started. The front flap of Elaine Yaffe's biography of my aunt states, "Above all, she is important because she was one of the first to perceive, and come up with remedies for, the ways in which American society was stifling women's aspirations and thwarting their achievements."

I was not foolish enough to try to match her achievements. During my first year of college, emboldened by my high school success in AP biology, I chose to tackle genetics. Sitting in the big lecture hall, I just couldn't follow the professor with his pointer as he barreled through explanations or grasp the detailed diagrams of cellular material. At the end of that semester, a "C-" glared out at me. When one of my older brothers heard about my grade, he said, trying to be cheery, "Well, at least we know that you won't be following in Big Polly's footsteps." Right.

I discovered, during my 20s and 30s, that measuring up to her wasn't the point at all: I could simply appreciate her for being a spectacular aunt. When I was a boarding schoolteacher, she offered the use of her New Hampshire farmhouse as a place where I could meet a boyfriend. Later, having tried to start a bold new chapter but stumbling instead, I landed in Boston without any job. She invited me to stay on the third floor of the home she shared with Dr. Clem Smith, her new husband, laughed with me as I weathered assignments from a temp agency, and then helped me gather furniture for a Somerville apartment. She knew what was going on, and that soon I'd be back on my feet. Sure enough, within a year I was wearing snazzy outfits to a job that lifted my spirits and dating the man I would marry.

She's been gone for twenty-six years. Now when I enter my study to write, sitting at a desk she gave me, I glance at that magazine cover and try to use my *own* brain as best I can.

Nobody calls me Little anymore—but she gets to stay Big.

Fannie Lou Hamer

By Gail Choate

I kill plants.

I don't mean to, but I struggle to understand what they need.

Once I had a hydroponic (un)Lucky Bamboo, but I forgot to water it; within weeks its leaves were brown and drooping. To make amends, I overwatered (okay, drowned) my Christmas cactus. Unable to face my failure, I banished the cactus outdoors to confront its destiny alone.

Three months later, the Christmas cactus stood tall, firm, defiant, and blooming.

How do some plants thrive against all odds?

Then again, how do some people?

One woman who exemplifies resilience in the face of adversity is Fannie Lou Hamer, a towering figure in the Civil Rights movement.

Born in 1917 in the heart of the Jim Crow South, Fannie Lou Hamer's life was deeply rooted in the bitter legacy of Mississippi slavery—ridicule, discrimination, and violence. Yet she refused to fade into the shadows of oppression. Instead, she emerged as a force for change. She served as the vice-chair of the Freedom Democratic Party, organized Mississippi's Freedom Summer, and stood steadfast against the DNC. Along with Gloria Steinem, Bella Abzug, Betty Friedan, and others, she co-founded the National Women's Political Caucus. Mrs. Hamer refused to wither. She grew. She blossomed.

The sweat of her enslaved grandparents and sharecropper mother was water to her soul. Mrs. Hamer's mother's efforts were never quite enough to fill the bellies of her twenty children, but her deeds nurtured their spirits.

> *My mother was a great woman. She went through a lot of suffering to bring the twenty of us up, but she taught us to be decent and to respect ourselves.*

Fannie Lou Hamer knew self-respect was embedded in voting, and she worked fearlessly to claim that right. It took three tries for the sixth-grade dropout to pass the Mississippi literacy test. When she finally did, Mrs. Hamer's decision to exercise her constitutional right to vote was met with violent reprisals from her sharecropper landlord, who issued an ultimatum: relinquish her right to vote or face eviction. Mrs. Hamer left her life and her family behind, but the racial violence followed her, and White supremacists sprayed her place of refuge with bullets.

> *The only thing they could do to me was to kill me, and it seemed like they'd been trying to do that a little bit at a time ever since I could remember.*

Mrs. Hamer could not escape racial violence even when she worked tirelessly alongside other Civil Rights activists. Once, authorities arrested her for nothing more than riding home from a voter registration workshop on a "wrong-colored Trailway bus." Racist jailers forced two male Black prisoners to sit on her feet and demanded they beat her near death with a blackjack.

> *If them crackers in Winona thought they'd discourage me from fighting, I guess they found out different. I'm going to stay in Mississippi, and if they shoot me down, I'll be buried here.*

Fannie Lou Hamer understood that fear, division, and violence are power's weapons. With them, whole assemblies of people are beaten, cast into the shadows, and left to die. For Mrs. Hamer, it would have been safer to stay in the weeds, keep small, and wait for someone to pluck her from her fate. But she didn't. She flourished.

> *We have to build our own power. We have to win every single political office we can ... just because this [person] is starting to show us a few teeth and talk nice doesn't mean he'll move over and let us have some of that power.*

Mrs. Fannie Lou Hamer stood up to power and demanded a place in the sun for herself and everyone society had cast aside. She understood that, as a nation, we are only as strong as the weakest among us.

> *Your freedom is shackled and chained to mine. Until I am free, you are not free either.... As we are all here on borrowed land, then we have to figure out how we gonna make things right for all the people of this country.*

As my resilient Christmas cactus defied the odds and lived despite my neglect, Mrs. Hamer sent her roots deep, rose tall, and bourgeoned. She lifted her face into the light of truth, dignity, and respect, and shone that light on injustice. Fannie Lou Hamer stands as a testament to the power of courage, resilience, and unwavering commitment to justice against all odds.

Margaret Sanger

By Kim Hanson

I don't actually remember *when* I learned about Margaret Sanger, but I do know that once I did, my life changed for the better.

At the age of 10, while attending Catholic elementary school, I watched families of six, seven, eight children struggle to stay afloat and knew there had to be another choice.

Years later I found myself working four blocks from the clinic named for the court case that made birth control legal in the United States. And the man I was dating (and would ultimately marry) was *born on the same date* as Margaret Sanger. Coincidence? Fate was pointing me toward a path that I still walk today.

Margaret Sanger's remarkable, fast, and (in)famous life is directly linked to what I and all women are facing today: We now live in a time where *Roe v. Wade* has been overturned. There are now twenty-four states with laws that seek to restrict birth control and abortion access. Political leaders are, once again, referencing the Comstock Act, which in the late 1800s made the distribution of contraceptives, or any information related to sex education sent through the mail, illegal.

How has that changed us—how has it changed *me*—and how do we remain active and vigilant in a time when concepts like feminist, social justice, and reproductive freedom have become unrecognizable? When state legislators are seeking to limit how, when, and if we become mothers?

Margaret Sanger's early career as a nurse in the 1912 tenements of New York gave her an unflinching view of poverty and the economically disadvantaged immigrants who continued to have children they could not afford.

The women in those families begged her to tell them how they could avoid multiple births. It was then against state law for Sanger to educate them on birth control. She did it anyway. There was a federal restriction against mailing family planning informational pamphlets. She mailed them anyway.

Her persistence and tenacity in telling the truth, in pushing reliable health information forward to make other lives better, inspires me. From her activism grew the organization we know as Planned Parenthood, which today provides safe, affordable health care to more than two million patients nationwide.

On my lunch hours I volunteered at that Planned Parenthood clinic close to where I worked and was happy to help share important women's health information.

Sanger's example taught me to speak up. Share useful information. Not to take no as an answer. Empower the powerless. Find allies. Ignore the naysayers and keep going.

I learned that it's not easy being a modern-day Cassandra—telling truth to power has its consequences. Margaret Sanger knew that as well. She was arrested numerous times, vilified in the press, and shunned in "polite" society for her outspokenness related to issues that were critical to people's survival but were considered immodest and immoral. She believed in such "shocking" philosophies as having every child be a wanted child and that every woman can and should be in charge of her own reproductive health.

More than a hundred years later, we are facing similar challenges related to women's autonomy.

I have witnessed three women I know make the extremely hard choice to end their pregnancies and am thankful that they were able to do so safely and legally. All three were supported by their physicians, partners, friends, and families. All three happened before *Roe* was overturned. I have nightmares when I think about what would have happened to each of them if they now lived in one of the US states where this choice has been legislated away.

So, how do we turn this around? Call your legislators. Advocate and vote for political candidates who support women's reproductive rights. Do these things over and over again until it gives us the equal rights that all women—all people—deserve.

This week, two of the biggest US pharmaceutical chains announced that they will sell the abortion pill mifepristone, with a prescription, in those states that allow it. They see a major marketing opportunity in today's unsettled political environment; we women see another lifeline for our sisters who need one, and breathe a temporary sigh of relief, even as the struggle goes on.

Margaret Sanger never gave up; I pray my generation and the ones behind it do not as well. We deserve the right to control our own bodies. There is no equality otherwise. In Sanger, we find inspiration.

Eleanor Roosevelt

By Courtney Baklik

Eleanor sits next to me at the breakfast bar in our kitchen. I type on my laptop and she picks up yet another book from her pile, a resolution in her pale, downturned eyebrows as she struggles to make sense of the groupings of letters on the blue page.

From the large, white windows we can hear her father raking the crisping leaves that have been drifting in a steady stream to the ground these last few weeks, a *crunch* as Eleanor's little brother lands in the pile that is formed. I think about the debris that will linger and affix itself to the skin under his fine, translucent hair and how, with warm lavender-scented water, I will scrub it away during his bath.

Eleven years ago, in a house I had rented for the academic season, I sat alone with a laptop. I had failed to obtain job offers from all the schools I had felt confident I would—the school I had attended, the school where I had interned, and others I thought would have happily accepted me as a teacher. I had a 4.0 GPA from graduate school, and I thought I had built relationships that would have secured me a position. But I had been wrong. So instead I accepted a job in a district more than an hour away from my friends and family, a place I hadn't heard of before and in which I knew no one.

At first, I was thrilled by the idea—a cottage a mere three-minute walk to the ocean. The fresh, salt smell of the sea was redolent in the air of the quaint beach community. But inside the house, the small windows let in little light, and the musty air smelled of the old woman whose soft, unaccommodating furniture still moldered in the home her children rented out following her death.

158

Feeling much like a ghost myself, I spent nearly all my free time inside the house. I had work to occupy me; I planned lessons and graded papers. There were also bills, which were new to me: the rent, the oil, my student loans, my car. I even paid the cable bill, though I couldn't work the ancient television set.

Instead, while I ate dinner I sifted through the limited viewing available on the internet in 2012. One night, I happened upon a documentary about Eleanor Roosevelt. Up until that point, I had only watched documentaries under duress in history classes, but something about this woman and her life captured my attention.

Eleanor Roosevelt was a woman who shouldered both her tragedies and responsibilities with grace and resilience.

In *The Eleanor Roosevelt Story* (1965), Pulitzer Prize winner Archibald MacLeish detailed Roosevelt's at times painful childhood, in which she lost both her parents and faced alienation from her family and her society. In spite of these challenges, she became the mother of six children, a First Lady, a delegate to the United Nations, chairperson of the commission drafting the Universal Declaration of Human Rights, and an outspoken, uncompromising champion of humanity worldwide.

So later that fall, when asked to chaperone my school's annual student trip to Washington, DC, I agreed. I hoped to fill my time with companionship and variety, both of which I was slowly finding as I strove to become more a part of the community, but I also wanted to return to a place I had visited several times before to see a woman I had overlooked on previous trips.

I found the rather plain, unassuming figure of Roosevelt that nonetheless captured her resolute expression and looked up at her, feeling my own strength, remembering her words: "What one has to do usually can be done."

And now I look at my little Eleanor and feel satisfied that, while I have not yet fulfilled a life's work, I have conquered the doldrums of loneliness that were the beginning of my adult life. I have aspired to be like Eleanor Roosevelt, "accept[ing of] a woman's responsibilities," in MacLeish's words. It takes a monumental sense of duty—one like Roosevelt's—to face womanhood, motherhood, a career while maintaining one's integrity and sense of self. But by channeling the strength of those women who have come before us, I believe that it can be done.

Geraldine Ferraro

By Pia L. Bertucci

In the 1960s Virginia Slims launched an ad campaign showcasing vignettes of women who had been restrained, not only from smoking in public but also from existing as human beings with civil rights. Their slogan, *You've Come a Long Way, Baby*, accompanied historically inspired counterpoints such as the 1975 ad featuring a nineteenth-century woman scouring an office floor captioned, "When a woman didn't have to run for office to be a public servant," or the 1983 spot in which women of yore ironed pants only men were permitted to wear. Despite the tobacco industry's agenda, these ads established a social-historical metric of women's advancement in American society, and resonated with women who were still effectively struggling for equal rights.

The Equal Rights Amendment was a hot-button issue when Geraldine Ferraro—the first Italian American to run for national office and the first female vice-presidential candidate for a major party—accepted the nomination at the 1984 Democratic Convention. The crowd exploded with enthusiasm chanting, "Gerr-y! Gerr-y!" But also, "E-R-A!" In that historic moment, everything seemed possible. However, as a stateswoman in the 1980s, Ferraro had to navigate a minefield of conflicting expectations: Be fierce but feminine, maternal but career-minded, attractive but not glamorous. And all these idealized characteristics needed to be reflected in her attire, a tricky challenge when there were no precedents. Ferraro, reflecting on that time, has stated, "There was no dress code for a female vice-presidential candidate.... I never wore slacks in public, of course."

Looking back on Hilary Clinton's 2016 signature look that launched a social media movement, "Pantsuit Nation," and the preferred attire of

Kamala Harris, it is difficult to imagine that a stigma was ever attached to pants-wearing-women. However, as of 2023, the ERA has yet to be ratified, and *Roe v. Wade* has been overturned.

Have we really come a long way, baby?

The answer to this question may lie, symbolically, in the encouraging words of Ferraro's own mother, inspired by their family name (*ferro* = "iron"). "You can bend it, but you can't break it. Go on."

This battle cry had served Geraldine well long before the historic nomination. The daughter of an Italian immigrant and a widowed seamstress, Geraldine Ferraro attended Fordham Law School at night while teaching elementary school by day. One of only two women in her class of 178, Ferraro graduated in the top 10 percent. She would go on to found and head the Special Victims Unit in the Queens District Attorney's Office. Eventually elected to Congress, she continued to fight for the marginalized and vulnerable while still, according to her daughters' accounts, flying home every other day in time for dinner. By the time she found herself in the national spotlight in 1984, Ferraro had proven herself resolute and unflappable, even in the face of intense scrutiny. Ferraro held her own through attempts by Ted Koppel, George Bush, and others to undermine her knowledge of foreign policy, and doubled down when asked by detractors to reconcile her pro-choice stance with her Catholicism.

From 1993 to 1996, as ambassador to the UN Human Rights Commission, she continued to fight doggedly for the oppressed, often negotiating treacherous patriarchal terrain. Ferraro boldly demanded redress for wartime sexual violence and effectuated the incorporation of women's rights into UN resolutions on human rights abuse.

Ferraro cared deeply about the causes she championed. Because of her, we have indeed come a long way, even if we experience one step back for every three steps forward. Ferraro's quote "Every time a woman runs, women win" is an encapsulation of her legacy. She may have lost the election, but she won a decisive victory. It was about more than shattering the proverbial glass ceiling; Ferraro validated the equality of women in the political arena and elsewhere. She was a role model for many women, including my 15-year-old self, whose other 1984 idols included Madonna, Princess Diana, and Mary Lou Retton.

Ferraro acknowledged that other female pioneers—the abolitionists, the suffragists, and the NWPC advocates such as Abzug, Chisolm, Friedan, and Steinem—paved the way for her achievements. In Ferraro's words, "We must not go backwards. We must and we will move forward to open the doors of opportunity."

Because of Ferraro, we have moved far beyond the question "Why not a woman?" for political office, and because of those who followed her, we will certainly never question a woman's desire to wear pants in public.

Dolores Huerta

By Michele Cardona

I've often wondered how, and if, one's given name predicts their journey. Is Felicity destined for happiness? Would Hope wind up optimistic? I've heard Hispanic names, and mentally translated them—I'd smile at the true meaning of girls named Alegria or Esperanza. However, when your first name literally means "pain" in your native language, should you be prepared for a lifetime of it?

Dolores Huerta was born in New Mexico in 1930 and grew up to be one of the most powerful women in American history. A champion of laborers, her name became synonymous with migrant workers and their struggle to unionize. It was Dolores who coined the phrase "*Sí, Se Puede*" ("Yes, You Can"), which has been used ever since to rally workers, and voters, to unite and believe in themselves.

Fueled by this name game, I can't help but think about Dolores. What would provoke a Hispanic mother to look at her newborn daughter and say, "Dolores"?

Dolores Huerta's story of heroism, courage, and activism was rooted in pain, but not only her own. From her beginnings helping her own single mother to her career as a teacher in New Mexico, Dolores seemed to have a radar that pinpointed the distress of others.

Long before the wine and singing at Coachella, the chants of the immigrant grape workers echoed loud and clear. Dolores heard their call and led the negotiation for the UFW and their workers to earn higher wages.

An agitator, that's what they called her. She made others uncomfortable by urging more people to protest. And Dolores doled it out—she made it *her* business to get into *their* business, to bother those who continually violated the rights of the farm workers. She took up this cause because, as a brown woman in the 1960s, she recognized the racist and unfair treatment of immigrants. She knew the cycle of abuse would continue until the workers stood up and said enough. They needed someone to unite them, to bring all their voices into one unified call to action. Someone who could tell them, "Sí, Se Puede"—"yes, you can."

The struggle became hers. Her own life was put on the line as well as she first aligned with the Filipino workers in their battle with agribusiness. She left her young children behind and went to Delano, setting the stage for the first of many battles. Uniting with Cesar Chavez, she worked tirelessly but rarely received affection, even when she received respect. On that end, she was forced to read the room—it was a primarily Catholic immigrant group she was defending, and they couldn't help judging Dolores and her life choices. What kind of woman leaves her children behind? What kind of woman has several husbands? More *dolor* awaits as she confronts that harsh reality.

Dolores fought relentlessly for these migrant workers, recognizing the similarities they shared with the Civil Rights and second wave feminist movements of the 1960s; she tried to align with them, focusing on their shared fight against a government that just did not want them to succeed. In the documentary *Dolores Huerta*, we see her desire to join Gloria Steinem, but her inability to reconcile with a woman's right to choose caused her confusion. As a Catholic, she struggled with some feminist ideas. Ultimately, she did get behind feminism, as she was literally becoming a face of that struggle. As a woman working tirelessly but seeing all her successes credited to Cesar

Chavez, it was a painful realization. Dolores, who had given up her life for others, was only seen as "Cesar's helper"—never his equal.

I've asked many Hispanic people why children are sometimes given such sad names. Soledad ("loneliness"), Piedad ("piety") and even Dolores—names that translate to suffering. It turns out there is a reason—it is a way to honor the anguish of the Blessed Mother, or Nuestra Señora de los Dolores. As someone who bore tremendous sorrow, many pray to her for strength while facing their own struggles. So these names have a special place in Hispanic culture for valid reasons, and perhaps a little "extra" help from above for the struggles that inevitably lie ahead is exactly what little girls need in this world.

Mary Harris "Mother" Jones

By Kelly Cecchini

I've been told I am an unusually strong woman. I have certainly weathered some difficult life events, but I'm not sure that makes me "unusually" strong. Determined, perhaps. Stubborn. At 42, I lost my 41-year-old husband. He had a heart attack, fell to the floor, and died. Breaking that news to his two adoring young children was the most difficult moment of my life. In the excruciating days that followed, I held it together because of those two kids. I *wanted* to fall apart, but I had to keep putting one foot in front of the other.

Mary Harris "Mother" Jones kept putting one foot in front of the other for ninety-three years despite losing everything. In 1867, when she was just 30, Jones lost her husband and all four of her young children to yellow fever in the span of a week. Utterly alone, she moved from Memphis to Chicago. She opened a dressmaking shop but lost it in the Great Chicago Fire of 1871. Talk about "unusually strong." This series of events would have destroyed most people, but Mary Harris Jones became Mother Jones, an organizer for the Knights of Labor and, later, the United Mine Workers of America. Jones "organized miners' unions in many states, [including] West Virginia, where conditions were most deplorable. She participated in the great strikes of the 19th and early 20th centuries, [and] she led the strikes against the railroad barons, the meatpackers, the steel magnates, the textile oligarchs, and ... the barons of coal" ("Meet Mother Jones").

In 1903 she organized a protest march of child laborers, many of whom had been maimed in workplace accidents, that led to popular support for national child labor laws. She was arrested more than once and served time. She was proud to be called "the most dangerous woman in America" by a district attorney and to be denounced on the floor of the US Senate as the "grandmother of all agitators."

How did she do it? How did "the most dangerous woman in America" carry on? From what bottomless quarry does that kind of strength arise? Is that kind of tenacity genetic? Or do we learn what we live?

Like Mother Jones, my ancestors fled the devastation of the Irish Potato Famine in the 1800s. My maternal grandmother, Mary Miley Cahill, had six children. When she was 51, her 62-year-old husband died. She cared for two terminally ill daughters for years before suffering an incapacitating stroke at 81. My mother was her full-time caregiver for two years.

My paternal grandmother, Grace "Mae" Boyle Sherman, also the daughter of Irish immigrants, gave birth to triplets in 1933. One did not survive the birth. Another died suddenly at 42. Only my father outlived Mae. When she died, my grandfather came to live with us, and my mother cared for *him* for four years.

My mother, Eleanor Cahill Sherman, had five children in eight years. She has otosclerosis which, coupled with a botched surgery, caused profound deafness in one ear and severe deafness in the other. Seven of us lived in a three-bedroom, one-bath house in New Hampshire, far from extended family. My father was often deployed. There was no money. I remember my mother sitting on the edge of her bed, counting out the change that would have to sustain us for another week until my father's US Navy paycheck arrived.

And yet my mother simply got on with it. My grandmothers simply got on with it. They kept putting one foot in front of the other. For eighty-eight years now, my mother has put one foot in front of the other.

Backbone. Mettle. Grit. That kind of dauntlessness: Is it nature or nurture? Perhaps it is both. Jones once famously said, "Pray for the dead and fight like hell for the living." She lived those words, enduring the unimaginable and then dedicating the rest of her life to fighting for others. She powered through devastating loss and went on to live a courageous and productive life.

Moxie.

Is it fair to compare the average person's ability to cope with that of Mary Harris Jones? She may well be the gold standard of endurance. In the face of great loss or hardship, though, we can look to the strongest among us for inspiration. We can dig deep to find what already lies within. And we can learn how to keep putting one foot in front of the other.

Maria Montessori

By Heidi Rockefeller

Dear Ms. Montessori,

You may think that I am writing to thank you for the impact your work has had on my career or in developing my own approach to teaching, but the greatest impact you have had on me was not in a professional setting; it was in my home.

Thirty years ago I graduated with a bachelor's degree in early childhood education. In textbooks I first heard of your philosophy on educating children with a play-based approach that highlights independence and autonomy. I carried your brilliance with me as I moved out of the classroom and brought your wisdom into my own family to illuminate my world and work as the mother of two children.

Only fourteen months apart, my daughters were always smart, funny, curious people who have grown into successful, self-reliant, compassionate, and interesting woman. Yet when they first arrived in quick succession, I was surprised how remarkably different they were from each other. In the space of a very few years, I was learning how to be a wife, and then a mother, and then learning to how to adjust to being the mother of two. It might have looked easy or at least straightforward in my college course and books on child development, but in real life it was complicated.

My girls' distinct ways of approaching the world from the moments they arrived in it made parenting them a challenge. And another challenge we faced in our small household was that I was struggling with bouts of depression. I am grateful that today's generation of parents can speak more openly about feeling overwhelmed, as well as about their personal mental health journeys. I often felt alone in my own struggle.

You were, Maria, a real help. Your philosophies for teaching children put tools into tool belt that helped me through some of the toughest days. I drew on what I learned from you about playfulness, independence, positive experience, and the delights of how children can experience life and learn from their own interactions with the universe.

The day we created an "I can get my own breakfast snack" shelf in the pantry was a wonderful illustration of how your philosophies shaped our homelife. There were some mornings when it was impossible for me to rise early enough to meet their energetic demands. So we set up a spot where they could get themselves something to eat in the morning. They grew so proud and confident, and it took enough pressure off me that I was able to get better so much faster, we decided to keep the shelf. It was both useful and a touch point of independence.

I even have photographic evidence of how well it all worked: Laura, age 3 or so in the picture, is feeding Abby yogurt from a cup. This small frame encompasses your influence in our home. Laura's confidence in caring for herself and her desire to help her sister shows (adorably, I should add) that encouraging my daughters to try to do things on their own, getting messy and learning by doing, was the way to make all of our lives more joyful and our family stronger.

You also influenced how my children learned table manners. My girls learned table manners through countless games of tea party and restaurant with me and their beloved grandmother, Mimi. It was a fun exploration of new ideas as their brains were busy absorbing all the lessons of polite behavior they needed to know. In contrast, my childhood experience was that children learned by rote, discipline, and correction. Without your influence, no doubt I would have taught my children the very same way.

I enjoyed parenting in this new, messy way. After one memorable birthday party, and with the whole extended family watching in trepidation, I decided to clear the dining room table and slather it in shaving cream, spray it with a bit of food-colored water, and cover the kids with smocks. As the parents watched their children "painting pictures" on my dining room table, their tension gradually transformed into amusement. That bit of messiness made for a great family memory.

"It is necessary that the child teach himself, and then success is great" is one of your basic philosophies—and you knew that would be messy. But if the price of messiness is both success and a shared bond? Then the experience is a gift.

Thank you, Maria, for giving the world, and me, your gift.

Nancy Pelosi

By Jeanna Lucci-Canapari

To: **jeanna.canapari@email.com**
From: **info@pelosiforcongress.org**
Date: **Every day, 10:38 a.m.**
Subject: **THE PRICE OF DEMOCRACY**

Jeanna, it's Nancy Pelosi. I'm going to level with you.

Don't delete this, please.

I have just learned from my Team that we have failed to meet yesterday's Critical End of Month Fundraising Deadline.

This is not good. We have not missed this deadline since January, when I accidentally confused a certain former president and the current one during a Fox News segment. In my defense, it was 6:30 in the morning in San Francisco and I had not yet had my latte.

But it's morning all over America now, [your name here]. So let me open the curtains and explain what's at stake if you and other Democrats don't **chip in $5—the price of one latte—before our next deadline at midnight tonight.**

Democracy, that's what.

While Dems are sitting around drinking lattes rather than supporting key battleground districts, He Who Shall Not Be Named is out there raising big bucks over his latest in a line of gaffes longer than his necktie. Remember when he confused me with Nikki Haley? That was a million dollars from South Carolina Republicans right there.

If you can kick in $10 before eleven p.m., Jeanna, I will go straight on Fox News and "accidentally" confuse Trump with Benito Mussolini. You know, the one who made the trains run on time. Oh no, wait, that's Joe Biden with the Amtrak. Sorry, I got them confused again. So, it's wonderful when he gets mixed up, but I can't?

To make myself perfectly clear:

I saw HIM try to OVERTURN an election HE LOST.

HE saw ME stand TALL while some MAGA NUT tried to overturn MY HUSBAND in the middle of the night.

I'm sorry, but again, was that fine with everyone? For that ... man, for lack of a better word, to raise money off poor Paul's banged-up head? Not for nothing, but if Paul had put that hammer away after I asked him to hang up that photo of me and Barack Obama from when we passed the Affordable Care Act, maybe this wouldn't have happened. Well, at least his care was affordable.

If you've been waiting for a sign to step up with $15, this is it, Jenny. Jeanna, I meant Jeanna. By ten-ish would be good.

As Speaker of the House—the first woman in the job—I, unlike some people, knew how to handle a hammer. I wielded that gavel like an Italian mother's wooden spoon. You understand, don't you Jeanna? You had an Italian mother, according to the census data I saw. So did I. We called her Big Nancy. When I saw Big Nancy with that spoon, I knew it was time to knock it off, right? That spoon said: Hey! Stop fighting with your brothers and come to the table! DC is the same: If I say, "Knock it off!" the Dems come straight to the table and fight for the American people. And by the way, WE know how to count. **If my math is correct, $25 before dinner would add up to flipping the House blue in 2024.**

174

I was tough, as Speaker. I didn't apologize. I got things done. And I'M "Crazy Nancy"? Come on. **Show him I'm not crazy by sending in $50 pronto. By EOB, if possible. No rush.**

"Crazy," he called me. The former president projects too much. Need I remind you that HE blamed ME for the January 6 insurrection? That's really sick. Me hiding under a desk in the Capitol with Schumer, while he's eating a Big Mac in front of the TV: That was my master plan. **You know, $100 would go a long way to fund my ACTUAL master plan: to rid the People's House of all of those who seek its ruin. I will bring them down and slow clap as I watch them go.**

Democracy isn't cheap, Jeanna. Neither are lattes. But I am not asking you to fund my lattes. I am not asking you to have my desk refinished after that hooligan insurrectionist put his feet on it. Hope he's enjoying his "tour" of prison.

$500. That's the cost of Democracy. For that, you get to keep the Bill of Rights. And if you sent it in the next hour, Jeanna, you would also get a copy of that swollen orange's 2020 State of the Union speech, personally shredded by me.

So, can I count on you, Janet?

Barbara Jordan

By Angela C. McConney

"We the People." It is a very eloquent beginning. But when that document was completed on the 17th of September 1777, I was not included in "We the People." I felt somehow for many years that George Washington and Alexander Hamilton just left me out by mistake. Through the process of amendment, interpretation and court decision, I have finally been included in, "We the People."

Congresswoman Barbara Jordan opened the Judiciary Committee's impeachment process against President Richard M. Nixon in 1974—providing a master class on the Constitution in one of the greatest American speeches of the twentieth century.

African American women have been the vanguard of American democracy, breathing life into the paper promises of the Constitution and expanding it to include rights for all. African American women have fought for the personal—their families—and for the national—the education, freedom, the franchise for people of color and women; justice, poverty, and democracy in the United States as well as throughout the world. The African American women's vote saved the US Senate from the indignity of Roy Moore and revived Joe Biden's presidential hopes, leading to Kamala Harris as his running mate and his promise to appoint an eminent African American woman to the US Supreme Court.

Barbara Charline Jordan—lawyer, politician, and scholar—forever strengthened the American body politic. She was a tireless advocate for civil rights protections for all Americans. At a time when women and people of color were excluded from government, she was a blueprint of "firsts" throughout her legislative career, being in "the room where it happened."

Ms. Jordan attended segregated schools and in the tenth grade she met Edith Sampson, an African American Chicago lawyer at Career Day. Ms. Jordan decided there and then that she would be a lawyer. Due to segregation, she could not enroll at the University of Texas at Austin, but she graduated in the 1956 inaugural class of Texas Southern University. She later graduated from Boston University Law School.

After losing Texas House of Representatives races in 1962 and 1964, Ms. Jordan won a seat in the Texas State Senate in 1966, becoming the first African American state senator in the United States since 1883. In her tenure as state senator, Ms. Jordan promulgated a minimum wage law, removed waiver of discrimination claims from business contracts, and established the Fair Employment Practices Commission. Elected president of the Texas Senate on March 28, 1972, she became the first African American woman to oversee a legislative body in the United States. In 1972 she became the first African American congressperson from the South since 1898, representing the eighteenth district until 1978. President Johnson mentored her, assisting in her appointment to choice committee assignments, including to the Judiciary Committee.

Ms. Jordan's three terms in Congress were prolific, and her opening remarks for the Judiciary Committee galvanize us now even as they did then:

My faith in the Constitution is whole. It is complete, it is total. And I'm not going to sit here and be an idle spectator to the diminution, the subversion, the destruction of the Constitution.

Following President Nixon's resignation, Ms. Jordan continued to advocate for civil rights protections for many Americans, expanding the Voting Rights Act of 1965 to include Latinx, Native, and Asian Americans. As the first African American keynote speaker at the 1976 Democratic National Convention (DNC), she stated:

A nation is formed by the willingness of each of us to share in the responsibility for upholding the common good. If one citizen is unwilling to participate, all of us are going to suffer. For the American idea, though it is shared by all of us, is realized in each one of us.

Why has Ms. Jordan captured a place in my heart and imagination? I too am an African American female attorney. I am grateful for Ms. Jordan's commitment to public service that maps a path where I may follow. I am humbled by her candor and her courage.

I conclude with a quote from her 1976 DNC address: "Equality for all, and privileges for none." It is painful that Ms. Jordan's speeches ring so true today, warning us against division in the face of eroding commonality. She has provided us with the pattern for true democracy, and rightfully stands in the pantheon of the greatest American leaders of the twentieth century.

Golda Meir

By Sherry Amatenstein

In 1969, as a 12-year-old marooned in Da Bronx, my fantasies of writing bestsellers, hosting talk shows, running for office—making my life count—seemed doomed. All the women in my orbit were, like my mother, Holocaust survivors—indomitable, but training 100 percent of their energy on being the perfect *balabusta* (Yiddish for "homemaker"). I didn't expect my family's summer in Israel to offer a different possibility for my future. Until a scalding night when I roasted uncomfortably in my nosebleed seat at Tel Aviv's massive Ramat Gan Stadium. I'd been dragged to this sweatbox for the Maccabiah Games—think Olympics. I watched Israel's new prime minister being driven around the field. She waved regally to cheers whose noise level probably rocketed to the Moon.

Back home, while watching me haphazardly skim the seemingly endless expanse of gold carpet blanketing our living room with our clunky Electrolux, Dad asked, "Are you dreaming about vacuuming the house for your husband, Sherila?"

Reluctant to upset a man who'd witnessed his parents and littlest sister (thankfully, two other sisters survived) led to the gas chambers at Auschwitz. I bit down the scathing comment aching to emerge from my throat.

Instead, I thought of Golda—who'd spent the first eight years of her life trapped under the boot of virulent anti-Semitic pogroms conducted by Kiev's Russian tsarist regime before immigrating with her mother and two sisters to Milwaukee, where her father, Moshe, was working as a carpenter.

At age 10, the then Goldie Mabowehz flexed baby activist muscles, creating a fundraiser to help needy students buy textbooks. Her efforts included renting a hall and putting on a show, during which the fledgling public speaker recited two Yiddish poems. A few years later, denied permission by her local synagogue to lecture within its walls about the importance of reestablishing a Jewish state in Palestine, she stood on a bench outside and spoke to congregants as they headed home.

In her 1975 autobiography, *My Life*, Golda disclosed how the anger she felt over her father's limited ability to protect his family from violence morphed into a "profound instinctive belief that if one wanted to survive one had to take effective action."

At age 14, effective action involved defying her parents' edict to marry a much older man and running away to join her married older sister, Sheyna, in Denver. Here Golda enrolled in high school and met politically and Zionist-minded Jews, among them her future husband, Morris Myerson.

While hero-worshipping Golda's "chutzpah," teenage Sherry couldn't muster the courage to resist my overprotective parents' insistence that their studious daughter attend a commuter college versus spending four years freed from their loving but suffocating bosom.

My parent-approved escape hatch was marriage to a 23-year-old pathological liar capable of leading a Master Class on the manipulation of 20-year-old naïve, gullible empaths. Walking down the aisle, I ignored my gut screaming, "Don't do it," and entered a union that proved emotionally and, occasionally, physically abusive.

Four years later we divorced. Despite knowing Jack was a spendaholic, I let him bully me into a do-it-yourself mediated split without protecting my separate financial assets. I got custody of our cat! When my ex declared bankruptcy, his creditors came after me.

Standing in a Brooklyn courtroom declaring insolvency before a brusque judge and my distraught parents was the tipping point that finally pierced my emotional paralysis, allowing my Inner Golda to scrabble her way into the light.

Rather than preventing my personal apocalypse, a lifetime of playing it safe and doing what was expected had left everything in shards.

Nothing was handed to Goldie Mabowehz; the pogrom survivor grabbed for what she wanted and bit off the head of anyone attempting to wrest it from her. Four years after I marveled at the then 66-year-old's triumphant spin around Tel Aviv's massive Ramat Gan Stadium, she steered Israel through the 1973 Yom Kippur War. This while suffering from the lymphoma that killed her four years later.

As a journalist, I've experienced life-changing adventures, including a performance at Radio City with the Rockettes and crawling into sewers in Romania to interview street children. I've also volunteered at Ground Zero, entered social work school in my 40s, and, more recently, refused to back down when my insurance company tried to deny me coverage for speedy (happily, successful!) treatment of the breast cancer that was diagnosed at the dawn of COVID.

I will never run a country, but thanks to my Inner Golda, nor do I run from worthy challenges.

Sandra Day O'Connor

By Cristina Cabral Caruk

President Reagan conducted a nationwide search for the first female Supreme Court justice and found Sandra Day O'Connor. Upon a unanimous confirmation vote to become first female Supreme Court justice, O'Connor said, "It's good to be the first. But you don't want to be the last." She served for twenty-four impactful and successful years, setting a necessary foundation for the female justices that would come after her.

When reading about O'Connor, I chose *First*, her biography by Evan Thomas, and *Lazy B*, her memoir named for her ranch in the Southwest. I realized that I share commonalities with her. We were both shy as young children, had gap-toothed smiles, and enjoyed reading Nancy Drew books. She was an only child until age 9, myself until age 7. We both worked with the law. I had a dog named Chico. One of O'Connor's favorite horses was named Chico. Like me, she had a father who was adoring yet dictatorial at times. We both had kind mothers who taught us never to speak ill of others. O'Connor's description of life at the Lazy B also reminded me of summers on my grandparents' farm in Portugal. O'Connor remarked that "one of the problems of living at Lazy B was the almost constant presence of flies." I too remember my grandparents' house had flies circling overhead due to the compost pile heaped a few meters from the house.

O'Connor's biographer described her as quiet yet confident, considerate, resourceful, and resilient. She had a blend of informality and dignity combined with charm. O'Connor grew up on a cattle ranch, and from these humble beginnings she thought it "did not seem possible to her that a ranch girl would grow up to serve on the highest court." According to *First*, O'Connor came from the West where folk had fewer airs. Her use of humor in speeches made everyone adore O'Connor. An example of her humor was when she said: "As my dear husband, John, used to say, you don't have to drink to have fun. But why take a chance?"

First described O'Connor as "straightforward, energetic and a born centrist." This "centrist" view is seen when she reaches across the aisle in a show of nonpartisanship. This is further evidenced by her hiring law clerks that were conservatives and liberals. In some cases she sided with the liberals; in others she voted with her fellow conservatives. She wisely knew how to compromise, and that made her the formidable "swing vote" on SCOTUS. She felt the role of the judge was to interpret the law, not make law. *First* noted that gender should make no difference as a matter of law, but that did not mean it did not make a difference as a matter of fact. Rejected by major law firms, O'Connor turned to private practice and then to electoral politics before her judgeships. She was the first female majority leader of the Arizona Senate and then a state judge prior to her nomination to SCOTUS.

O'Connor and I had other similarities. When she took a new job, she suffered a bout of anxiety. I suffer from anxiety myself. "Sitting all day in a soap opera" is how O'Connor described her time as a trial judge. She also struggled with rigorous treatment for breast cancer and never missed a day in court during that time. I too was diagnosed with cancer; however, mine was of the thyroid, and thankfully I recovered and am able to work. When asked how she took care of her family and still had a career, O'Connor answered: "Always put your family first." As a result, she resigned from SCOTUS when her husband's health was failing in 2005. Once again, I have found a kindred spirit in O'Connor, because no matter how much I enjoy law, I also put family first.

O'Connor was held in high esteem. She received honorary degrees and lifetime achievement awards. She was recognized with the highest civilian honor, the Presidential Medal of Freedom, which President

Obama bestowed on her. Arizona State University boasts the Sandra Day O'Connor School of Law. I am most impressed by two facts: First, O'Connor did not sacrifice her family's best interests to advance her own career. Second, in her role as associate justice she was empathetic to the plight of women, children, and minorities. I had the privilege of paying my respects to her while she was lying in repose this past December 18th, having passed away at 93.

Ruth Bader Ginsberg

By Sophia Gabriel

Ruth Bader Ginsberg is my sorority sister. Alpha Epsilon Phi, Cornell 1950. Even though we were 68 years apart, and even if we weren't tied together by rituals and songs, I would still call her a sister—most women probably would. When someone fights for your life to be taken as seriously as the man sitting next to you in your office, at the grocery store, or at the head of your dinner table, it's a safe bet you'd care about them like you would your own blood, despite never meeting.

We seem to think that there is a basic, common understanding among society about the rights of human beings; what they mean, who they apply to, and when they're violated—until there isn't. I thought when I told the skinny blond boy in the back seat of my car "No," he understood me, until he didn't. I thought I still had full control of my body when he pulled my ponytail and asked me if I liked it, until I didn't. I thought I could wear a dress on a first date because I thought I looked pretty until I couldn't, because he thought the hem being above my knees meant his hands could roam freely and question my choice in underwear, making me apologize for them not being sexy enough. I've apologized for that pair of underwear a few times now. The second time was at the police station two days after the first. "No, Officer, the underwear I was wearing has been washed already, I'm sorry."

When basic understandings of the rights of human beings, including women, became undone, blurred, or simply not taught to begin with, at least we had Ruth. A powerful soul pioneering a mission to educate the world, and release women. And when education wasn't enough, or the words "No," "Stop," or "Help" were disregarded, she was someone sitting on the bench that looked like *us*, understood *us*, and empowered *us.* She also made sure the twelve members of the jury, responsible for deciding if we were victims or not based on the amount of alcohol we drank, looked like us too.

When the government didn't entrust women with decision-making regarding our bodies, at least we had Ruth. She made sure my life was always taken as seriously as a life being carried inside of me. Especially when that life threatened my own or wouldn't live long enough to know the world for its truth. Ruth Bader Ginsburg stopped the vehicle that is my body from being driven by and for men to reach an agenda that's not my own. When and where I became the passenger on that car ride are two things I don't remember agreeing to, just like the ketamine put into every one of the drinks bought for me at the bar from a gentleman in Gucci loafers. But at least we had Ruth.

RBG was *the* presence in the US government who made me feel that if someone touched me without my consent, I wasn't crazy when I wanted to scream. I wish she was the judge I got to speak to at the police station, not one who looked around for the victim, thinking he was in the wrong place when he didn't see someone beaten up or fitted with a cast. Ruth would've known that some bruises bleed interminably on the inside, only for me to see.

Now she's gone, and even when she was here, she couldn't save all of us. No one can. When RBG was put into her grave, many of us started sinking, succumbing to the wave of power and strength that, without her, seems to build everyone up *except* us. Like the waves that keep hitting the boats tied to the dock in the water, that never truly stop coming even when the ocean seems calm. One or two always sneak in on account of their stature or perceived lack of strength. The boats thrash against the water, sometimes succeeding against the infinite power of the currents, sometimes turning over completely, face down, until another wave decides to flip them over again. Thankfully, some docks stand tall enough to thwart the incessant waves so the water cannot rise above them but finding those docks seem ever fewer and farther between.

Ruth Bader Ginsburg ignited a raging fire that burns in the souls of millions. Burns through entitlement, and hate, and words like "You must've been asking for it." Thank God we had Ruth.

Janet Yellen

By Elizabeth Norton

By the first anniversary of my mother's death, soon after what would have been her 101st birthday, I'd made some progress sorting through her stuff. I brought to a consignment shop things I hadn't wanted but couldn't quite part with—what she'd call the Scarlett O'Hara pile ("I'll think about that tomorrow"). Mom always said she saw whole rooms from her life in such shops, as women her age went into nursing homes or died. Now I'm seeing her actual things. Her orangey watercolor is still there. I've considered buying it back. It goes with an armchair upholstered in oranges, but I'm forced to admit I don't want that either.

I'd also read a biography of Janet Yellen, not because I'm interested in economics, but because she's from the same neighborhood as my mother and me—Bay Ridge, in Brooklyn. Yellen is not only the first woman, but the first person to be chair of the White House Council of Economic Advisors, chair of the Federal Reserve Board, and secretary of the treasury. Whereas my mother said the nice thing about turning 90 was that she figured she could stop worrying about what she wanted to be when she grew up. She earned a science degree from Barnard but sacrificed nursing school to marry my father. Retiring at 85 from her law firm job, she wished she'd become a lawyer.

As an undergraduate at Brown, Yellen aspired to work at the Federal Reserve. In college I didn't know the Fed lends money to failing banks, but I'd seen *It's a Wonderful Life*, when James Stewart tells the angry depositors the money isn't in a vault, it's invested throughout the community, and Donna Reed saves the day by waving their honeymoon cash. In 2008 Fed Chairman Ben Bernanke, playing Donna Reed, rescued securities firms from collapsing under bad mortgages.

It was Yellen who explained to then–Senator Obama that the ensuing global meltdown was a bank run writ large.

Nor did I know that between panics, the Fed uses interest rates to balance the economy. The legendary Alan Greenspan steadied an overheating economy to a classic "soft landing," raising rates in 1994 enough to reduce inflation without causing a recession. Yellen steadied Greenspan, advising cuts in 1995 when things cooled, since high interest discourages spending and borrowing, driving up unemployment.

I couldn't have less in common with Yellen professionally. I wanted to be a writer. My college, Sarah Lawrence, didn't require majors. A few interesting science courses led to a science writing career, which fizzled during my caregiving years.

But when the seventy-eighth US secretary of the treasury remembers her childhood, she sees the same landmarks I do. She lived near Owl's Head Park on the Narrows, with gracious trees and views of Manhattan and the Verrazzano Narrows Bridge. She'd know the concrete playground, covered with gravel, the steel swings on rusty chains. The 69th Street pier, where I went with my grandfather and still see whenever I hear Otis Redding's haunting "Dock of the Bay."

Yellen and I learned to love reading in the same library, all blonde wood, windows, and light. Nearby, two streets end in cliffs, with staircases for pedestrians. For me these had the mystery of the lamplit steps of Montmartre. Up on the ridge, a Victorian castle lifts its spire. When Yellen thinks of high school, she must remember the house across the street made of loaf-shaped stones set into mortar, with an undulating roofline that follows the hill. A house where a wizard might live.

Am I seeing through her eyes or she through mine? I couldn't wait to leave Brooklyn—my heart was in the country—and it's startling to remember I found those places magical. I seem to have made a soft landing of my own. My mother was so ready to go. A year later, having emptied her house and made some headway with the boxes in mine, I'm letting go too. Letting go of attachments—to things, to what I assume

I should be. I've completed a third novel. Two weren't published, but I did get a good agent. I've taken a computer science class; I might start a YouTube channel for women learning to code. Interest rates are high, but Yellen says inflation is coming down, the labor market strong. She hopes for another soft landing.

Sometimes I feel free of the need to "be" anything. And I'm not going back for that orange painting. I'm casting ominous glances at the chair.

Anne Bonny
& Mary Read

By Carole DeSanti

By his Excellency **W O O D E S R O G E R S**, Esq.; GOVERNOUR
of New Providence, & c. **A P R O C L A M A T I O N.**

> "Whereas John Rackum, George Featherstone,
> John Davis, Andrew Gibson, John Howell, Noah
> Patrick and *two Women, by Name*, Ann Fulford
> *alias* Bonny & Mary Read, *did on the 22nd of*
> August *last, combined together to enter on board,*
> *take, steal and run-away with … a Certain* Sloop
> *call'd the* William, *… and with the said* Sloop *did*
> *proceed to commit Robery and Piracy.*"

In late October 1720, pirate hunters spot the *William* off Jamaica's
coast. An exchange of gunfire ensues, but capture proves difficult.
While most of the crew disappears, two hold the decks with uncommon ferocity—determined, capable, and fearless. When, late into the
night, powder and lead exhausted, they are forced to capitulate, the
ship's defenders are found to be the two women named in the warrant:
Anne Bonny and Mary Read.

At the height of piracy's so-called "Golden Age," England is bent
on defending its commerce in sugar, molasses, wood, and especially
its routes between Africa and the Caribbean that carry enslaved labor.
The crew of the *William* is carted off to Spanish Town for trial, its men

sentenced to death and hanged. Afterward, their bodies are strung over the harbors on gibbets: a warning.

In their separate trial ten days later, the women, like their comrades, appear defiant as their crimes are read out: *That they did feloniously and wickedly, consult, and agree together ... to plunder and commit robberies and murders on the high seas.* Indeed, Mary Read is claimed to have later said, "As to hanging, it is no great hardship. For were it not for that, every cowardly fellow would turn pirate and so unfit the sea, that men of courage must starve." (Anne's famous line, reportedly spat out to Rackham, the ship's captain and her lover, was that if he had fought like a man, he wouldn't have to hang like a dog.)

The prosecution's witnesses, former captives aboard the *William*, all state that Bonny and Read wore trousers and male garb; were not kept by force but of their own free will; that they cursed, swore, handled guns and powder, and in all ways appeared equal to their fellows. One witness, a woman, Dorothy Thomas, says they threatened her with death for fear she would speak against them in court, and bared their breasts—her only indication of their sex.

But after Bonny and Read are convicted and sentenced to hang, in a feat of turning justice and gender identities upside down, both women enter a plea of the belly—claiming to be pregnant and quick with child. By law, their executions are stayed, and they are sent back to prison to wait out their terms.

Mary Read dies there the following spring, possibly in childbirth. Anne Bonny disappears, and then vanishes from history.

What little we do know about the two comes from the 1724 compendium *A General History of Pirates*. This volume tells us that Anne, born in Ireland, was the bastard daughter of a lawyer and his housemaid, the three then immigrating to the Carolina colonies. That before running off to sea she injured a young man for "trying" her and was rumored to have killed a servant girl. That Mary Read, born near London, was raised as a boy by her widowed mother (to ensure support from a relation); joined the army, married a soldier, and for a time ran an inn in the Netherlands. Upon her husband's death, and again in disguise, she shipped out as a sailor. Apocryphal tales include Anne becoming smitten with the cross-dressing Mary Read, and that, in a separate matter of the heart, the swashbuckling Read dueled a crewmate and won.

The *General History*'s sources are mysterious. It may be partly, or largely, fictional; its author, Captain Charles Johnson, was possibly an alias of Daniel Defoe. Pirate tales themselves are famously mash-ups, fiction indistinguishable from facts; screens on which we project dreams of liberty, escape, defiance, even utopia. Read and Bonny have come down to us as cartoons, caricatures, and fantasies—hoydens, heroines, and pirate queens—as both lovers of men and as lesbians.

A marker stands at Ireland's Old Head of Kinsale, a wild and windy spot, claiming to be Anne's birthplace. A grave in St. Catherine's Parish, Jamaica, is said to be Read's. But as to their reasons for going to sea—whether they were friends, lovers, or something else—we can only imagine. How did they live aboard ship? What enabled Anne's escape, and where did she go? It's left to us to imagine. But that's the lure of the pirate—and why they carry us into the realm of the dream.

Queen Maeve of Ireland

By Niamh Emerson

When I was 5 and my sister was 3, my parents took us on an adventure. We climbed to the top of Queen Maeve's grave, or cairn, located on the top of Knocknarea, a mountain in Sligo, Ireland, our hometown (it's a mountain, not a hill). Mom packed snacks, and Dad filled us in on the legend of Queen Maeve. My sister and I were very excited—about the snacks (for my '80s Irish babies, she packed "Postman Pat" sweets).

What we remember about that adventure is:

- It was a beautiful day, where sunshine hit every crevice of Sligo and you could feel the warmth in your belly.
- We laughed a lot. I don't remember what was funny, but the sound of the four of us laughing is one of the first things that comes to mind when someone mentions Queen Maeve.
- As the story goes, if you're going to visit Queen Maeve's grave, you had to bring a stone with you to add to the top. We spent an especially long time picking just the right stones, as toddlers are wont to do.

But who was Maeve? What did she do to merit a cairn on top of a mountain?

I bet you know a Maeve, or know someone who knows a Maeve, or have heard of a Maeve. I would also bet that you, or someone you know, once described Maeve as feisty, or fiery, or "a force of nature."

Have you ever heard a man called "feisty" or a "force of nature"?

Maeve, or Medb, Meadhbh, Meabh, and Meibh, was the Queen of Connacht (potato–potahto / Maeve–Medh). Described as the "fair-haired wolf-queen," Maeve was so beautiful that when a man looked at her, he lost two-thirds of his valor.

Maeve's father, the High King of Ireland, married her off to her first husband, but after giving birth to a son, she was done with THAT guy. Maeve's father kept her busy, however, by removing Tinni mac Conri as king of Connacht and making Maeve queen of Connacht in his place. Maeve had several men in her life, and at one point made it known that her mate should be without fear, meanness, or jealousy.

Ancient mythological queens—they're just like us!

Queen Maeve is best known for starting the Táin Bó Chúailngné, or the Cattle Raid of Cooley. One day, Maeve and a new husband, Ailill mac Máta, were having a simply delightful debate on which of them was wealthier. They went back and forth, with Maeve reminding Aillil that she was a warrior queen in her own right, defending Connacht and commanding armies long before Aillil came into the picture. They were evenly matched—except for Aillil's prized bull, Finnbheannach. Maeve, livid, decided to procure an even better bull. The only bull in Ireland that could match Finnbheannach was Donn Chúailgne in Ulster. Maeve made an honest attempt to buy the bull outright, but at the very end of the negotiation, the bull's owner reneged.

Maeve decided to take the bull, Donn Chúailgne, by force—by the proverbial horns. A battle between her army and the men of Ulster ensued, and Maeve cursed the men of Ulster with the pains of childbirth (she had nine children of her own; she knew exactly what she was doing). Her brilliant move was short-lived, as Cuchulainn, one of Ireland's greatest warriors, single-handedly fended off her army. But in a plot twist, and to make a long story short, Cuchulainn allowed her to take the bull back to Connacht. Donn Chúailgne fought and killed Finnbheannach, but later died of his own wounds.

Maeve and Aillil went on to fight more battles and keep up their sparring matches. Maeve was eventually killed by her nephew, who was seeking revenge for Maeve having killed his mother, who was also her sister. Using a slingshot, and after practicing for several weeks, he killed her (with a piece of cheese—but that's another story).

Maeve was buried standing up, facing her enemies in Ulster, ready for battle.

The lesson from Maeve? The next time you go to call a woman fiery or feisty, ask yourself if she's the feisty enough to go to battle over a bull, or fiery enough to curse her enemies with the pains of child-birth, to be buried standing up, and to be feared even in death? That is a force of nature I can celebrate, a woman deserving a cairn, and a picnic, and a legend.

Temple Grandin

By Laura Rockefeller

My entire childhood I seemed "off" to the adults in my life. I thrived on routine and struggled when plans changed. I hyper-focused on niche topics to the exclusion of all else. I hated hugs and making eye contact. I couldn't pick up on social cues or empathize with my classmates. I was in my own world a majority of the time, and in some respects I loved it, but I always longed to be understood.

It wasn't until fourth grade that a teacher suggested I get tested for an autism spectrum disorder. I was simultaneously relieved and burdened by my new Asperger's label. I had always known that I was different, but now the fact that I was different was confirmed by a medical professional. At the time of my diagnosis, ASDs (autism spectrum disorders) were not nearly as recognized as they are now, and it felt as though every dream I had for the future was shattered; that is, until I watched *Temple Grandin*.

I remember sitting in my grandparents' living room as a middle-school student watching the latest Claire Danes movie. She was portraying Temple Grandin, a celebrated animal behaviorist and academic. What drew me in was seeing someone like me represented on the big screen. Temple Grandin served as living proof for me that even though my mind works differently, I am still capable of incredible things. My journey might not match that of my peers, and I may face additional obstacles, but that is okay.

Claire Danes's presentation of Temple Grandin broke the "autistic robot" trope all too common in Hollywood. For the first time I saw someone like me, whose expression of empathy is nontraditional, but by no means nonexistent. It's Temple's empathy for animals that has made her so successful in the livestock industry. She recognized patterns in their behavior and temperament, along with getting on all fours herself to see things from the perspective of cattle. Using her observations, she developed a more humane system for the slaughter of livestock still widely used today.

Looking back at my own childhood, I'm reminded of how my empathy manifested itself. I always liked to think I had a special connection with our family cats, but I think the reality was that I envied their worry-free existence: home all day with the same four people, and the ability to hide at a moment's notice when things got uncomfortable. My empathy was more focused on people. I found myself particularly drawn to my neurodivergent classmates. They were more forthcoming with their emotions. They would vocalize exactly how they were feeling. There were no guessing games, just plain language and usually a paraprofessional to guide interactions. When it came to my neurotypical classmates, it took a while for me to comprehend how they were feeling based off their facial expressions or body language. When it clicked that a friend was upset or hurt, I was quick to spring into action. I displayed empathy through overwhelming generosity with my time, money, and resources. This is one quality I still pride myself on to this day.

It's been sixteen years since I received my diagnosis. I served as president of my high school class. I earned my bachelor's degree in business administration. I got married. I found my passion. I've been told by a number of professionals that my Asperger's diagnosis does not make sense today. Regardless, Temple Grandin's story gave me the hope I needed during my formative years to aspire to greatness. The label no longer matters, but I continue to see Temple Grandin's profound impact on my life.

Malala Yousafzai

By Maria Parenteau

We are only a year and three days apart in age, Malala Yousafzai, and yet you've been an inspiration and a leader to myself and people of all ages for most of your young life.

You have always presented yourself to the world with poise, grace, and bravery. You fought for women's right to education in this way, even when you first began to do so at the young age of 11 by blogging and informing the world about the misogyny and volatile destruction the Taliban was inflicting upon your village in Pakistan. And after an assassination attempt on your life in 2012, at only 15 years old, the whole world learned your name. I remember hearing on the news about a teenage girl on the other side of the world who took on a terrorist group that, in an effort to stop her from fighting for equality in education and women's rights reform in Pakistan, tried to kill her. You were shot in the head and placed in a medically induced coma for ten days, but you survived. Not only did you survive, but you also fought back, proceeding to do even bigger and greater things to empower women on a global scale by co-founding the Malala Fund with your father. At age 17, you were even named the youngest person ever to receive a Nobel Peace Prize. I know the passion and commitment you have to this worthy cause will only propel you to continue to do astounding things.

But sometimes I wonder, maybe even you have been afraid before too. Were you scared of retaliation? Were you worried for your family's safety? I think maybe you were fearful at times, but you chose to accept that fear and be brave regardless of its presence in your heart.

You chose to take a stand even when it may have been the hardest thing you had ever done.

And then I wonder: What created that spark inside you? Do we all have that spark? Do we just need to choose to see it in ourselves and choose to act on it? Because you chose to fight. But you chose to fight with peace and with your mind, setting an example for all the young women. You wanted to have the right to education and for every other girl be able to claim that right as her own.

I want to fight like you, Malala, with decorum, dignity, and strength. A beautiful combination of what a woman is and what she can do. You bring new meaning to the analogy of "like a girl." To fight like a girl is to fight tirelessly, relentlessly, and courageously for good. A glow from the spark inside of you shines bright and guides us all to a place where we can see the reflection of that spark within our own hearts and minds. Maybe every little spark in each of us is what we can use to illuminate the good in humanity.

Bethany Hamilton

By Margaret Anne Mary Moore

Until age 24, running seemed permanent in my routine. Born with cerebral palsy, I grew up using my walker to run alongside able-bodied peers on cross-country and track teams. My enjoyment of athletics overshadowed the health benefits. Without physical activity, people with CP risk muscles atrophying and the cessation of bodily functions.

Running's impact was illuminated when pneumonia dealt me a stay in intensive care and a yearlong recovery. I was prescribed an eight-week hiatus from exercise, then had to gradually regain the lung capacity necessary for running. Pausing the workouts that keep CP manageable, constant pain sliced across my body. Doctors correctly projected running as the cure.

With the walker surrounding my body's front and sides, I pounded my feet against the outpatient clinic's floor. Every few minutes a therapist measured my oxygen using a pulse oximeter. I had been used to three-mile courses. Now dizzy with a 30 percent oxygen drop after fifty feet, I was whisked to my wheelchair. This weekly routine lasted eight months.

"At your first race after recovering ... ," my mother said following one session.

"I don't think I'll run another 5K," I sighed.

As an established motivational speaker, positivity was my specialty, but the rigor of recovery was draining me.

"You can't give up."

Exhaling, I wondered how many attempts I'd make before walking successfully.

Before my next session, I found myself watching *Soul Surfer*, a film about Bethany Hamilton losing her arm in a shark attack, defying odds and becoming an award-winning surfer. Unable to push herself from a lying position to stand on her board without a second arm, Bethany believed her surfing career was over. Her father eventually installed a handle onto the board, which allowed her to maintain stability while repositioning. Bethany's experience inspired me to consider additional measures—coordinating breathing with leg movements—I could take to walk successfully. My motivation returned for my next therapy session.

"I want to try walking again," I said.

The therapist refused, suggesting I stretch instead, and continued to do so for weeks, despite my mother's and my protesting. While recovering, I was restricted to walking under medical supervision. My therapist's unwillingness brought immense frustration.

"I was hoping you'd walk again," she finally said. "But that's probably not possible."

Since doctors insisted on my running, her comment was easy to brush off but was still alarming, making me worry about how I'd proceed.

As the therapist spoke, my mother grabbed her iPhone and ordered a pulse oximeter. We later received doctors' approval to walk at home.

I wonder if the non-movie Bethany laughed in relief upon realizing her father's plan as I did with my mother's. We started with slow walks with frequent oxygen checks.

"Looks good," my mom exclaimed. "Feel okay?"

"Yeah," I beamed. "Let's keep going."

There's a scene in *Soul Surfer* where, post-recovery, Bethany's dad shows her several surfboards. "You're here," he gestured to a "beginner" board, then to the advanced. "We need to get you here." A video montage follows, showing Bethany struggling then succeeding in workouts. This resembles my own experience.

"We need somebody who can create a fitness plan to get you running normal distance," my mom remarked.

Seeing an advertisement, I applied to Gaylord ParaTriathlon program, which offered summer training for an autumn triathlon. With my coach now my personal trainer, I found myself walking around a vacant lot. Twenty minutes in, my oxygen plummeted, signaling my need to sit.

"If your oxygen's okay after twenty minutes," he said at our next run, "Can you try more laps?"

I agreed and increased the distance each week.

"You just ran three miles in forty-five minutes," my coach exclaimed as fall approached.

"I've never run that fast," I gaped, remembering my fifty-eight-minute best.

Competing on a relay team at my first race, I sprinted across the finish, grinning. Never having qualified for awards, I was shocked to be announced as winning the disability division.

At my second race, I was the second-place individual disabled finisher.

Beaming and accepting my prizes, I couldn't believe I had returned as a stronger athlete.

I often ponder what to do with the wisdom gained from my experience. Perhaps Hamilton's words provide guidance: "I wouldn't change what happened to me because ... I wouldn't have this chance ... to embrace more people than I ever could have with two arms."

From my pain and perseverance came more strength than I knew I had. Now, like Hamilton, I share my story to help others discover their power to become champions in ways unimagined.

Tammy Duckworth

By Lara Meek

Come, let me tell you the tale of Senator Tammy Duckworth and how she defeated a man whose ego was three sizes too large.

In 2016, doomscrolling Facebook, I came across a video clip titled "Mark Kirk Questions Opponent Tammy Duckworth's American Heritage at Illinois Senatorial Debate." As a biracial woman, being "American" enough is a topic I was all too unwillingly familiar with. I watched as Representative Duckworth gave an impassioned speech about the dangers of rushing to war because she knows the cost. That she's a member of the Daughters of the American Revolution, and she herself has served and bled for her country, as has her family since the Revolution.

When Senator Kirk was given a chance to respond to her cautions of war, he instead decided it was a good idea to imply that she was a liar. His response: "I had forgotten that your parents came all the way from Thailand to serve George Washington." My mouth dropped open, and years of rage from being told I'm not American enough boiled up. I felt ready to take off my earrings and defend this woman I didn't know—a loyalty I usually only reserve for strangers I've met in a women's bathroom line after ten p.m. I watched as Senator Kirk gawked at her, waiting to see if he had gotten under her skin. I wanted her to rip his head off, but I know that's not an option if you are a woman, especially if you are a woman of color. Show anger, tears, or raise your voice slightly defending yourself, and you have lost the argument, according to some unknown rulebook.

I waited for her reaction, but there was none. She sat looking forward, waiting patiently, not looking upset in the slightest. When she was asked if she'd like to respond to Kirk's remarks, she laughed cheerfully and offered an upbeat "Sure!" It didn't sound like she was laughing at him; it was more the kind of laugh you have right before explaining to a child why they can't have ice cream for dinner. (You're not mad; you just understand that they don't know any better.) She recounted her father's family during the Revolution, and how her mother immigrated to America from Thailand. That she is proud of both of her heritages. Kirk lost the debate—and then the election.

After watching the clip, I researched Duckworth. I learned she's an Iraq War veteran, losing both legs when the Black Hawk helicopter she was in was attacked. That she was the first female double amputee from the war, and that after losing her legs, she continued to serve in the Army National Guard for another ten years. It would seem her opponent had failed to do even a brief Google search of this woman before their debate. But he did know that she's a congresswoman, a fellow solider in the Iraq War, and a double amputee. All this was not enough to stop him from confidently calling her a liar on live TV because she's visibly biracial. I sat back in my chair and took it in. If Tammy Duckworth isn't American enough, what shot did I have?

Throughout my life, I was never White enough, Hispanic enough, and certainly not American enough—even though all my grandparents were born on US soil. Boyfriends' mothers complained that I wasn't a "normal" American girl.

That day, I went from not knowing who Tammy Duckworth was to feeling that, for the first time in history, I could actually be represented in Congress. And Senator Duckworth then did just that, fighting for reproductive rights, immigration, and changing the rules of the Senate floor to allow children under one to be present during voting for breastfeeding. Later she became the first US senator to ever cast a vote while holding a baby.

Duckworth helped me realize that the bar is so high to be considered a real American, it's a relief to realize that it's actually just made up.

People disagreeing with me politically like to bring up the wars their family have fought in, never contemplating that my family has been fighting wars for America for the last hundred years.

I hope I can channel Senator Duckworth next time someone questions my heritage, and that instead of instant fury, I can just give a chuckle and say, "Sure!"

Katherine Dunham

By Adrienne Lotson

Sunrise in Bali.

As a 16-year-old Dartmouth College student, in the seventh class to admit women, my college journey was often fraught with isolation and the search for community. When an Afro-Caribbean dance class was offered one winter term, I jumped at the opportunity, hoping to find a space for creativity and belonging. I always loved dance, even if it did not always love me. My parents could not afford ballet lessons, so I enrolled in the free ballet classes offered to "inner-city" kids in my town. The instructor continually made clear that because of the shape and size of my body, I would never succeed as a dancer. My body did not resemble or move like a real (i.e., White) ballerina, she would tell me. My butt was too big. My hair could not be slicked back into a tight bun. I did not belong. Although I may have loved the way my body felt when I moved, ballet was about conformity, and you, dear Adrienne, never could—and, thank God, never would—conform. With this dance trauma engraved on my body, yet with eager anticipation and hope for something different, I walked through the giant doors leading to the dance stage.

"Okay, students, welcome to the Katherine Dunham method. In today's class you will use eight beats to cover the floor with a grounded hip sway. On the eighth beat, you should arrive at this spot on the stage; this is your mark. That is the structure of the movement, but remember, Dunham's method prizes freedom: freedom of movement, freedom of thought, freedom of purpose. Freedom within a structured form! Embrace who you are, embrace how your body moves. Be true to yourself. Remember, your goal is not to look like anyone else. Don't try to fit in. BE YOU!!! Just make it to your mark. Now, 5, 6, 5, 6, 7, and ..." What? Don't try to fit in? Be true to your own body? Be free? Authentic, yet within a structure? Have an idea about where you are going and a generalized path to getting there, but be free to adjust, to do what feels right and find joy in the process? Little did I realize that Katherine Dunham was about to profoundly impact my life.

When discussing the pantheon of dance greats, Dunham's contemporaries, dancer-choreographers George Balanchine and Martha Graham, are immediately heralded as changing the trajectory of dance in America through their eponymous techniques and schools of dance. Often overlooked, or outright ignored, Katherine Dunham's technique and school of dance, which elevated the place of Caribbean and African movement in modern dance, created an equally seismic shift in the cultural landscape. Her impact, however, was not limited to the dance world.

Dancer, choreographer, social activist, and Hollywood star, Katherine Dunham was also one of the first Black women to receive a degree from the University of Chicago's renowned anthropology department, having studied with the legendary Melville Herskovits. It was there that she married her artistic acumen with the worldview of a scholar. Founder of the academic discipline of dance anthropology, Dunham called upon her ethnographic fieldwork throughout Haiti, Jamaica, Martinique, and Trinidad to infuse her choreography and technique with cultural significance. She recognized, celebrated, and promoted the echoes of African dance, movement, and ritual embedded in the dance forms of African diaspora cultures in the Americas. The African worldview of individuality within community, exploration with adjustment, and celebration of one's uniqueness would permeate her Dunham's work and become a guidepost for my life.

True to Dunham's method, in that Afro-Caribbean dance class there was a place for everyone, regardless of height, weight, flexibility, training, gender, rhythm, or look! All that mattered was that you take the discipline seriously and grow. We would repeatedly learn about her concept of freedom within a structured form. Discipline was important, but it did not translate to sameness, rigidity, or loss of personality. Movement was about honoring your body and what brought you joy. The goal was not to be like anyone else, but rather to utilize the resources around and within you to construct and implement your best form. That class, and all those I took thereafter, laid the foundation for my life's mantra. To have an idea of where I was heading but be free and flexible in how I get there. Dunham's mantra has seen me through careers as a pioneering sports attorney, global storyteller, minister, women's retreat leader, and administrative law judge. Most delightfully, I too have become an arts-focused cultural anthropologist, having earned a PhD at the age of 55.

Today, as I sit in Bali watching the sun begin its daily dance across the Balinese Sea, I am overcome with amazement and gratitude. I wonder if my 8-year-old self, sitting in her favorite tree yearning for a life of adventure, could have foreseen that the lessons learned in a seven a.m. dance class would equip her to set out on her structured form—a path of service to improve the lives of women globally. A path where she would embrace as her life's mantra the freedom to be bravely authentic. An authenticity that would lead her to embrace myriad careers, travel to more than sixty countries, and take advantage of opportunities to impact lives globally. Finally free. Freedom to not conform. Freedom to be me. Freedom to follow my bliss. Freedom in a structured form. I found my freedom and belonging thanks to my guiding star, the great Katherine Dunham.

Diana Rigg

By Esther Cohen

I have long admired the late Dame Diana Rigg, but admiring an actor is complicated, isn't it? Because what, exactly, is one admiring? There's the esoteric question: How can one separate the artist from the art they create? Or, watching a play or film, what are you responding to when you see a great performance?

More to the point, though: What was I responding to whenever I saw Diana Rigg perform? The character as written? The director's vision? The emotional honesty and dedicated professionalism she brought to her work? How can I describe the intense, emotional connection I felt every time I saw her?

I think I had a crush on Diana Rigg.

At the time Dame Rigg died in 2020, she was a storied actor of stage and screen. Working continuously for more than sixty years, she was lauded by her peers and appointed a dame by Her Majesty the Queen. She performed in Shakespeare and on *Doctor Who*. She was James Bond's only wife in the 1960s and the malevolent Lady Tyrrell in *Game of Thrones* in the new millennium.

And she was strong and opinionated, quitting her first television role over gender pay inequality: a lonely and controversial stance at the time.

I first saw her when I was a preteen, watching late-night television. In my house in the 1960s, no one paid any attention to what we watched after ten p.m. on a Saturday night. I'm sure my parents never even knew that my brother and I had discovered *The Avengers*.

210

It had everything an overly dramatic 12-year-old could want: tart, sly British humor; double entendres in every scene; bowler hats and afternoon sherry; John Steed, the suave, ever-resourceful British spy; and his partner, Mrs. Peel.

As played by Diana Rigg, Mrs. Peel changed something in me. She was young, sexy, and 1960s London-stylish. She was a scientist, spy, and expert fencer. She didn't need to be rescued; often she ended up rescuing Steed. She was brilliant and insightful, and looked damned good in spike-heeled boots. And while I may have been gobsmacked by Mrs. Peel, I was smitten by Diana Rigg.

As a kid, I was always drawn to plays and movies and was considered pretty theatrical by my family (not necessarily a compliment). I understood, intuitively, that I was drawn to the stage, and often surprised my working-class family with my relatively exotic interests. Why would 12-year-old me insist on watching the Royal Shakespeare Company's film of *A Midsummer Night's Dream*? I certainly didn't understand the story. But seeing Diana Rigg play the jilted, devoted, often-foolish Helena was, for me, a bolt from the blue.

At that time, I hadn't been exposed to performers with the training and range of British actors. I had no understanding of how one actor could make my heart leap while playing so many different roles. Diana Rigg, like her characters, was someone I hadn't yet imagined or understood—an actor with not just talent but also training, dedication, and emotional range.

Diana Rigg was proof to me that theater could be both a passion and a life. And, unlike her characters, someone who inhabited a world that might, just might, be attainable for me.

I saw Diana Rigg on stage twice, the first time in 1978. At the time, it wasn't hard for a broke drama student to find cheap theater tickets in London. But Diana Rigg was performing in the cheesy classic *The Guardsman*, and I couldn't resist. I wanted to see Rigg perform live. I was not disappointed. Rigg was playful, cheeky, and cunning. Mrs. Peel all grown up, and in period costumes.

And years later, Dame Rigg solidified her place in my heart, playing Mrs. Higgins in *My Fair Lady* on Broadway. Now a grande dame of the stage, she could have sailed through the performance with a wink and a nod. Instead she brought a gravitas to the character that I had not seen in other productions. Mrs. Higgins is wiser than the men around her and, as played by Rigg, recognizes Eliza Doolittle's savvy and unrealized potential. Despite being initially disdainful of the girl, Mrs. Higgins turns out to be compassionate, intelligent, independent, resourceful: someone who lives within society but can think beyond its mores. The right role model for Eliza.

From the first moment I saw her on television until the last time I saw her on Broadway, Diana Rigg was the grown-up I wanted to be: talented, sexy, intelligent, outspoken.

Claressa Shields

By Ash Carrington-Manning

Dear Ms. Shields,

Before you became a legend as a boxer and mixed martial artists, you were a dinosaur—even a monster. You were an unknown, unclassifiable creature—angry and loud, vicious and violent.

I learned, when discovering you and reading about your background, that we shared the same childhood: We shared the same destructive, abrupt rupture of our innocence. You were in Flint, Michigan; I was in West Haven, Connecticut. We both lost our voice for a couple of summers. Then, dormant for so long, you erupted. At 17 I saw you roaring and fighting, standing your ground in your own body.

You were powered not by a rage but by a strength I had only seen elders possess. Your spirit was captivating and inspiring. I studied your training camps—your battles with various corporations for recognition.

As I shadowboxed with you from afar, looking into my mirror and seeing you there, I could begin to feel myself breathe again, fully. Begin to breathe myself into being; breathing myself strong, seeing myself strong.

I saw your ascendancy, pioneered only by you—seeing you as another fighter, with a loud mouth and a community to keep herself safe. My voice and sense of self grew with sessions in training camp. As sporadic as training was, it helped me learn the fundamentals.

You have accomplished the impossible repeatedly; over and over again, you triumph and let your admirers know what it takes as well as what it means. I am writing this to you to let you know that I see you. I see you not only as a two-time gold medalist nor as the only woman to hold all four major world titles in fewer than ten fights, but as a woman who told her story the best way she knew how—by getting into the ring.

There is no "if you were a man, or White, or more feminine" scenario to be spun when we talk about your career. There simply is the present in which every Black woman built their blood, sweat, and tears to continue the fight. Our fight. Every woman knows it, but not everyone survives it. From me to you, I ask that you never stop fighting.

Sincerely,
A Fellow Fighter

Nancy Wilson

By Sharon Bailey

My parents amassed an impressive stash of blues, R&B, and jazz albums over the years. When I was a little girl growing up in the '70s, the first thing my father did when he got home from his automotive assembly job was kiss my mother and me, walk over to the large Magnavox console stereo that sat alone along a wall in our apartment, and put on one of our favorite vinyl dreams: Dinah Washington, Marvin Gaye, Aretha Franklin, Miles Davis, Ella Fitzgerald, or maybe John Coltrane.

Listening to music floating through the air while my mother fixed dinner was the perfect complement to her delicious cooking. Relaxed and happy, suppertime was a meal for the senses. But if I heard Sarah Vaughan or Carmen McRae, I knew one of them was riding a wave of guarded emotion. It could be joy or sorrow. It could be ignited by anything or anyone. As the kids say, they were "feeling some type of way." Whatever they were going through, only "Sister Sarah" or "Sister Carmen" could fix it.

One day, my father came home with a new album. I asked him if I could see the cover (I was still too young to touch an actual vinyl record). He gently placed the large, square cardboard sleeve into my outstretched little hands. On the cover was the prettiest Black woman I had ever seen. Seated on the floor against a white background and dressed in an elegant long, golden yellow pleated skirt, she flashed the most dazzling smile. The woman on the cover was Nancy Wilson. The album, aptly titled *but beautiful.*, made perfect sense. She *was* beautiful.

Seeing the excitement in my eyes, my father lifted the arm and placed the shiny disc beneath the needle. I sat on the floor, like Ms. Wilson, and stared at the cover. Her gaze seemed to look right through me. With a voice as sweet and smooth as honey, she sang, "Love is funny, or it's sad," the first line of the album title track. And just like that, I understood how my parents felt. The next year, my parents took me to see her perform at Kleinhans Music Hall. I was 6 years old. I knew from that moment, only her voice could help me handle life's boomerangs.

From that moment, whenever I felt a budding romance, a breakup, a new adventure, or one of life's upheavals, only Nancy Wilson could fix it.

When I was 13 I fell in love with a very handsome boy whose family had recently joined our church. The very sight of him left me paralyzed and mute. He was my first crush. I was not his. Wilson's "Save Your Love for Me" helped me through my first experience with unrequited love.

Against my mother's wishes, I went to college out of state. Anticipation grew as I started my college to-do list with Ms. Nancy belting, "No one knows better than I, myself, I'm by myself alone." My journey into adulthood began almost four hundred miles away in Washington, DC—where I knew not a soul—with the song "By Myself" as my North Star.

My mother fought hard yet lost her battle against cancer, one month shy of my parents' fortieth wedding anniversary. I was 31. My father, blind and heartbroken, died a few years later. Time never completely heals emotional wounds. Sometimes, the pang of grief comes out of nowhere and hits you hard. It's one of those boomerangs in life. Whenever I think of them, I give in to my sorrow and let Nancy assuage my sadness with "When October Goes."

Several years later, a friend of mine, a talented cellist with the Buffalo Philharmonic who was aware of my deep admiration for Nancy Wilson, graciously presented me with a ticket to her performance, once again at Kleinhans Music Hall. As a bonus, he also invited me to a meet-and-greet following the show.

I was an emerging vocalist myself. No longer in possession of the original *but beautiful.* LP, but armed with a CD, I stood in line to meet my idol, my love coach, my fairy godmother, Nancy Wilson.

She smiled and autographed my disc while I told her that her music was the soundtrack for my life. And just like that, she looked right through me, stretched out her arms, and gave me a hug.

Elizabeth Taylor

By Elena Greenberg

Before there was RBG, Judge Judy, or Nancy Pelosi ... there was Liz! My childhood fascination with Elizabeth Taylor has shaped the woman I've become...I never consciously wanted to be a movie star, but I always wanted to be an independent, self-confident career person, calling my own shots within my personal and professional life.

And as a child of the '60s, the famous women I saw growing up were all movie stars—and I knew my movie stars. My parents were film buffs, and for as long as I can remember, they took me with them to see the features at the local theaters. My mother was a stay-at-home mom, and when I came home from school, one of our favorite pastimes was watching the 4:30 movie together. While others were watching *Dark Shadows*, as a preteen growing up in the 1970s I was watching the stars of the '40s, '50s, and '60s in between the endless commercials on the *4:30 Movie* (on ABC from 1968 to 1981), which replaced the *Million Dollar Movie* on our local New York television channel.

My mother's favorite actress was Elizabeth Taylor, and I knew why. They had the same coloring and the same outspoken persona. But nobody, not even my mother, could compare to Taylor's glamour. My mother did not admire many women, but Taylor had it all: the looks, the fame, the jewels, and the ability to tell a man where to go without worrying, even for an evening, about finding an immediate replacement. Liz Taylor was a mother, a lover, and the most famous woman in the world.

My mother may have exposed me to this icon of the screen and stage, but being an avid reader and researcher, I became fascinated with the roles she played—a "party girl" (*BUtterfield 8*), a demented Southern belle (*Raintree County*), a jetsetter (*The V.I.P.s*), an artist (*The Sandpiper*), and, most impressively, Queen Cleopatra, a role for which she demanded and received a million-dollar paycheck. In those days, no other women were insisting on million-dollar paychecks. To make matters even more interesting, as she was playing the Queen of Egypt, this unofficial queen of Hollywood dumped her wimpy fourth husband and fell in love with her leading man, English star Richard Burton (with whom my mother was equally enamored).

My mother wasn't the only one.

During the 1970s, Taylor and Burton were the most famous and enchanting couple on the planet. They were splashed across the gossip pages daily; the diamonds, the yachts, the drinking, the brawling—no film could be more exciting than their actual life together. The day I found out they were divorcing, I was bereft. I took it personally.

But like the goddess Persephone, Liz returned from the underworld every time folks thought she was finished. The gossip outlets repeatedly proclaimed her gone. But in Taylor's case, she'd reappear, not with a new season but with a new film (which later turned into a new "cause"), a new style, and, almost always, a new man. I looked up to her in the same way I looked up to Scarlett O'Hara; she was unapologetically a triumphant survivor—and she looked damn good doing it!

As a second-year law student in the early 1980s, there were not very many female attorney role models for me. Taylor remained my idol as a bold, brash, brilliant businesswoman (who always got the best of her husbands in divorce). And so in June 1981, at the end of my second year in law school, I finally got the chance to see my idol live on Broadway in Lillian Hellman's play *The Little Foxes*. I was probably one of the few 24-year-old fans she had at that time, so I wasn't surprised that no crowd of autograph-seekers gathered outside the theater on that hot June night. I was simply happy to be the one standing there. Friends who saw the show with me were impatient and just wanted to get home, but they knew how much it meant for me to see my idol in person. And so we waited. And waited. Finally, dazzling but dressed down in a purple tie-dyed blouse and jeans, Liz Taylor appeared. She smiled at us, thanked us for coming to see the show, and then drove away in her stretch limo.

Since I was a teenager, one of my favorite Liz Taylor's lines has been "I'm Mother Courage. I'll be dragging my sable into old age." I don't know why I always liked that quote, particularly since old age seemed so far away at the time.

Now I know.

Marilyn Monroe

By Amy Sherman

Marilyn: Can you believe it? It's been more than sixty years since you left us. You and your iconic works remain frozen in time, but you were ahead of yourself, and the world has not yet caught up.

It was Ella Fitzgerald herself who declared that you were ahead of your time. I wonder how she felt when you supported her singing, her performance, her art, by promising a club owner that you would come to both of Fitzgerald's shows every night. You publicly and privately championed the artistry of other women—and people of color—when those in the entertainment industry marginalized them. Before people discussed "social justice" as part of cocktail party conversation, you were helping to enact it.

You would be devastated to know what happened to the Kennedy brothers. Not that your relationships with that family were uncomplicated. Your liaisons with the Kennedys were concealed to avoid scandal; only you know whether that was what you wished. But there is no privacy for anyone in the public eye now. Famous people are shown no mercy. But scandal? It isn't always the kiss of death anymore. A sordid dalliance with a porn star, for example, cannot stop a grotesque man from getting elected to the highest office. Is that freedom? Is that progress?

In 2009 some of us believed that we were seeing progress and that things were looking up. We elected Barak Obama, a Black president. Imagine singing "Happy Inauguration, Mr. President." You would probably have chosen a different dress and been less breathy in your delivery, but you would still have captured the moment in triumph.

And you might have hoped, as many of us did, that having a Black president would diminish hatred in our country. Not so much. White nationalism in America runs deep. We are still as divided as we were in 1963. We could use the power of your voice and influence today.

You would appreciate the fact that there has been a modicum of success in getting some serious women's rights. Oh, women aren't treated equally—don't be ridiculous. It's only the first part of the next century. But a mere decade after you left, women earned the right to be in charge of their own bodies and reproductive choices. A real game changer.

You would have been amazed.

Emphasis on "*would* have been."

What was written into the Constitution fifty years ago, guaranteeing women choice, is currently under assault. Women's rights are under a new and formidable attack. Our very existence and justifiable cries for equality are being met with an iron fist by conservative people who run parts of our country. Religious patriarchy has its boot on our necks, trying to return this country back to the 1950s.

Maybe this would not surprise you. If anyone understood the tyranny of insecure men, it would be you. I worry that our country is turning itself inside out trying to squelch people's freedoms to be who they are, love who they want, and express their desires. The current climate would remake your revered classic film into *Some Like It Not*.

But get this! Something significant happened in Hollywood, of all patriarchal places: Women in the film industry stood up to sexual assault by some of the guys who run the business. It prompted a "Me Too" movement: "Me Too," referring to the fact that there isn't a woman alive who hasn't had a story about inappropriate men using their power to force women to compromise themselves or alter their lives because of them.

Remember when you said, "Hollywood is a place where they'll pay you a thousand dollars for a kiss, and fifty cents for your soul?" All those mixed messages are alive and well, but women gathered our voices together and were finally heard.

Finally, there's a new technology called artificial intelligence that can visually bring you back from the dead. Without your consent, of course, because when did consent matter, right? I've even had my face morph into a version of yours through AI filters.

But artificial intelligence is exactly what it sounds like—fake smart. It cannot bring back the brilliant, caring, beautiful soul of you. I laugh at the irony of artificial intelligence trying to mimic the artificial ignorance you so deftly played in some of your funniest characters.

Marilyn Monroe: More people want to be you than *you* ever wanted to be you. You remain, however, singular, brilliant, and imitable—frozen in time but alive in our imagination.

How Fay Weldon Taught Me to Be a Writer

By Gina Barreca

Fay Weldon did not teach me to write, but she did teach me that I could be a "writer": a professional who puts sentences on paper with the goal of achieving recognition and getting paid.

A formidable figure in the world of arts and letters for fifty years, Weldon (born in 1931, died in 2023) wrote the opening episodes of *Upstairs, Downstairs*, thereby creating what would become the classic Masterpiece Theatre legacy of British dramas being exported to the United States. She was the author of *Life and Loves of She-Devil*, *Female Friends*, *Letters to Alice: On First Reading Jane Austen*, *Praxis*, *The Shrapnel Academy*, and dozens of others. Weldon was awarded a Commander of the British Empire for her contributions to arts and letters, was chair of judges for the Booker Prize, and received a basket of honorary doctorates.

Novelist, essayist, journalist, playwright, and screenwriter Fay Weldon was everything I admired: original, smart, wicked, witty, conspicuously hard-working, and breathtakingly generous to the community of readers she gathered around her.

I became part of that community in 1979, when I was student at Cambridge University. Weldon's novels were everywhere in England. I bought *Remember Me* at a bookstall in King's Cross railway station and didn't look up once during the journey back to college.

Weldon's authoritative, incisive, bitter, funny truth-telling captivated me. I read everything of hers I could find.

Five years later, focusing my scholarly work in part on her fiction, I learned that Weldon was stigmatized as "too commercial" to be taken seriously. Her frequent appearances on television, radio, in print magazines, and in tabloids were at odds with her increasingly well-respected literary work. Yet her New York publishers thought she was not commercial enough to spring for a reading in the United States.

A woman writer was either too famous or not famous enough? Really?

That seemed unreasonable. Typing on blue airmail stationery, I sent her a note explaining I'd secured funds to invite her for a keynote. Confessing my own academic interest in her writing, I was also quick to reassure her that I wouldn't be digging up her garden to look for unfinished manuscripts.

Weldon answered immediately. She wrote, "By all means dig up the garden. You can keep the manuscripts. We shall plant bulbs."

I nearly swooned, and I am not the swooning type.

Weldon's first American appearance was at Queens College. The auditorium was packed. Her New York publishers and agent, seeing the standing-room-only crowd, doubled the print run of her next novel. It snagged the front-page of the *NYT Book Review*.

Weldon's influence was profound, in part because she took positions on current events and declaimed—often in hilarious ways—on everything from nuclear war technologies, stepchildren, the collapse of British banking, fast food, cloning, reincarnation, diets, every conceivable (and inconceivable) kind of sex, and publishing. She came to the aid of Salman Rushdie when he was under a death threat and, perhaps as dangerous, defied initial popular resentment toward

Camilla Parker Bowles, now Queen Camilla, by arguing that two adults who loved each other should be allowed to marry.

Weldon, who has her protagonists burn down houses and attempt to clone their ex-lovers, is not defined by postmodern cynicism but writes, "To the happy all things come.... . It is our resentments, our dreariness, our hate and envy, unrecognized by us, which keeps us miserable. Yet these things are in our heads, not out of our hands; we own them. We can throw them out if we choose."

What Fay declared during that first trip in 1984, when I was eyeing in a store window a pair of red heels I couldn't afford, was that I "must write books." She said, "It's what I've done."

She hoisted up her designer handbag as proof.

Knowing it wouldn't be easy, Fay also warned me for the next thirty years that writers risked being misread or misunderstood. Reflecting on her own fame in 2020, Fay wrote to me that "Distant readers may admire me for my sense of humor, though I hope those closer recognize the fragmented, melancholy, dysfunctional soul behind the laughter-raising facade (though I fear not)."

With her works translated into over forty languages and having taught, lectured, and dazzled audiences worldwide, Fay's exuberance, honesty, and inspiration tilted the world slightly on its axis.

Readers have been digging up Fay Weldon's garden for years, recognizing that she planted for us a complexly beautiful plot, famously sown with wild oats and filled with encouragement. Fay Weldon gave us an ideal place for us to choose our own words, so that we might, without fear (thinking of red shoes), begin.

About the Contributors

Sherry Amatenstein, LCSW, is a NYC-based psychotherapist, author, anthologist, and longtime journalist. Sherry has written for many publications, including shondaland.com, AARP's *The Ethel*, the *Washington Post*, *The Cut*, *Next Tribe*, *Hadassah*, *Tablet*, *Good Housekeeping*, and *Better Homes and Gardens*. She runs workshops on overcoming trauma and female empowerment. See more at howdoesthatmakeyoufeelbook.com or X @SherapyNYC.

Wrote about: Golda Meir
Golda Meir (1898–1978) served as the first and only female prime minister of Israel.

Luisana Duarte Armendáriz is a children's book author, translator, and English PhD candidate at the University of Connecticut. Her academic research interests include the exploration of such topics as home, intercultural and intergenerational relationships, religion, and language in contemporary children's literature.

Wrote about: Salma Hayek
Salma Hayek Pinault (b. 1966) is an Emmy-nominated actress and producer.

Anne Bagamery is a journalist based in Paris. She grew up in the Detroit suburbs and graduated in 1978 from Dartmouth, where she was the first female editor in chief of *The Dartmouth* campus daily. A former senior editor of the late, lamented *International Herald Tribune* in Paris, her work has appeared in *Forbes, Institutional Investor, Savvy, Worth*, the *International New York Times*, Vogue.com, the *American Lawyer*, and *Persuasion*. Her essay "Clean Copy" appeared in *Fast Fierce Women*; her essay "Feminism and Mom" appeared in *Fast Fallen Women*.

Wrote about: Sally Ride
Astronaut and physicist Sally Ride (1951–2012) was the first American woman to embark on a space expedition.

Sharon Bailey, a beacon of journalism from Niagara Falls, New York, stands out as the sole Black weekly opinion writer for a daily newspaper in western New York. Her impactful perspectives embellish the *Niagara Gazette* and *Lockport Union–Sun & Journal*, even extending to CNN.com. Outside her journalistic endeavors, she's celebrated as the "Rhythm Queen of Western New York," consistently earning the title of "Top R&B Female Vocalist" at the Buffalo Music Awards. In her leisure time, she relishes tranquil e-bike rides and hiking adventures with her partner, Tom.

Wrote about: Nancy Wilson
Nancy Wilson (1937–2018) was a Grammy-winning singer of blues, jazz, R&B, and soul.

Courtney Baklik is a high-school English teacher, but considers parenting her two children her real career. She and her husband have lived and worked their entire lives in Connecticut. Courtney appreciates the comfort and community of the small towns that hold a special place in her heart. She completed her undergraduate degree as well as two master's degrees at the University of Connecticut, which is, more importantly, where she studied writing with Gina Barreca.

Wrote about: Eleanor Roosevelt
Former First Lady of the United States Eleanor Roosevelt (1884–1962) was a politician, diplomat, and activist.

Gina Barreca has never been famous enough to be upgraded to a better seat, not even Economy Plus, not even on a small regional carrier. Or on a bus, for that matter. It's not that she's bitter. Gina was, however, in the excellent company of Fay Weldon at JFK when Fay was upgraded to First Class on a British Airways flight to Heathrow, so she knows it can happen. This photo of Fay and Gina was taken in Fay's home during the summer of 2012.

Wrote about: Fay Weldon
Fay Weldon (1931–2023) CBE FRSL was an author, essayist, and playwright.

 **Judah Berl** is a graduate of the University of Connecticut, with a BA in both English and Chinese. A three-time nominee for the Connecticut Poetry Circuit, Judah has been published in *Connecticunt* and performed at numerous events. While Judah's work does serve to put herself on paper with the hopes of reaching an audience that can relate, her biggest ambition in writing is to actually go inward, to find a relating audience within. She feels her duty as a writer is to help other people see and feel seen, even if that person is herself.

Wrote about: Sylvia Plath
Sylvia Plath (1932–1963) was a poet, novelist, and short-story writer best known for *The Bell Jar*.

 Originally from Chicago, **Pia Bertucci** relocated to the Carolinas to pursue a doctorate in Italian from the University of North Carolina at Chapel Hill. Currently she is the director of Italian at the University of South Carolina. Pia's other publications include "Baba's Mirror" in *Fast Fallen Women*, "Middle Sister" in *Fast Fierce Women*," her novel *Between Milk and India*, and various publications on Italian language, literature, and food culture. In her free time, Pia enjoys food-centered travel, attending Toad the Wet Sprocket concerts, and relaxing with her husband, children, and two dogs.

Wrote about: Geraldine Ferraro
Former US Representative Geraldine Ferraro (1935–2011) was the first woman to be nominated for vice president by a major political party.

Patricia Wynn Brown is a writer, speaker, performer of humor memoir, and dancer. Her new memoir, *Royal Roots: Reimagining a Life*, arrives in 2024. She has volunteered performances and classes, and has also advised a women's health project (this in conjunction with the Ohio State University Medical School) for the inmates at the Ohio Reformatory for Women since 2015. Her favorite response from the incarcerated women is "You make me feel like a human being." A reaction she received after her Hair Theater Shows, performed across the country for fifteen years, was "I needed that laugh more than you will ever know." Stories and humor are her medicine too.

Wrote about: Patti LaBelle
Patti LaBelle (b. 1944) is a soul and R&B singer-songwriter.

Linda Button feels a kinship with Lizzie Borden, thanks to the cadence of their names, identical initials, and dark yearnings for retribution. Button's writings have appeared in the *New York Times, Longreads, Huffington Post, Cognoscenti*, and on NPR. She's a black belt in Tae Kwon Do and loves her sprawling, complicated family with abandon. Want more Lizzie? Read Cara Robertson's brilliant, exhaustively researched *The Trial of Lizzie Borden* and take a bonny trip to Fall River to better understand the US justice system, a woman's changing place in the world, and Lizzie Borden's acquittal.

Wrote about: Lizzie Borden
Lizzie Borden (1860–1927) was famously tried and acquitted of the axe murder of her father and stepmother.

 **Jeanna Lucci Canapari** is a freelance writer in Guilford, Connecticut. Her freelance work appears in Yale University publications, and her personal essays have appeared in *Salon*, *Creative Nonfiction*, *Allegory Ridge*, and *Off Assignment*. She holds an MFA in creative nonfiction from the University of King's College (Halifax, Nova Scotia) and BA in English from Columbia University. Though she is originally from Long Island, she has been known to tell people she is from New York City or, just vaguely, "New York." She is currently at work on a memoir centered on the intersection of truth and mythology in an Italian immigrant family.

Wrote about: Nancy Pelosi
Politician Nancy Pelosi (b. 1940) is the first woman to serve as Speaker of the House.

 **Michele Curry Cardona** studied English/creative writing with Gina Barreca at CUNY Queens College in New York. Their bond was immediate and the impact lifelong. While working as publicity director for a NYC publisher, Michele won an essay contest that literally changed her life. After staying home to raise her children, Austin and Gabriella, Michele returned to graduate school and earned her masters of science in education. Currently she is an English language arts teacher in middle school, enjoying every minute in the classroom.

Wrote about: Dolores Huerta
Civil rights advocate Dolores Huerta (b. 1930) is one of the most influential labor activists of the twentieth century.

Ashaliegh "Ash" Carrington is a writer, educator, and mentor based in New England. She has written for Teagle Humanities Fellowship, Long Wharf Theater, and Woodhall Press. Nominated for the 2022 Pushcart Prize for her work *Black People Don't Do This*, Carrington continues to use her work to bring forth conversations on multiculturalism, intersectionality, and identity.

Wrote about: Claressa Shields

Boxer Claressa Shields (b. 1995) is one of only three boxers in history to hold all four major titles in the sport.

Cristina Caruk is a Portuguese immigrant and award-winning attorney auditor in the insurance industry. She graduated from UConn Law in 1991 and worked as a litigator for more than twenty years. She contributed to the flash nonfiction anthology *Fast Fallen Women*. She also authored a short story "Christmas Comes Early," featured in the anthology *Joseph, You Take the Baby!* She is married with two children and has one grandson. She has admired Justice Sandra Day O'Connor for many years and was honored and humbled to write about her in the current anthology.

Wrote about: Sandra Day O'Connor
Sandra Day O'Connor (1930–2023) was the first woman to serve as a US Supreme Court justice.

Nicole Catarino is a Connecticut-born poet, translator, and writer. She is an alumna of the University of Connecticut and graduated from Louisiana State University with a master of information & library science in 2023. Her writing has appeared in the *Hartford Courant, New Square Journal, Long River Review*, and *Women's Media Center*, and she was also a contributor and editor for the previous Fast Women anthologies: *Fast Funny Women, Fast Fierce Women*, and *Fast Fallen Women*. She currently works as a public service assistant at a public library, where she finds a new love for library science every day.

Wrote about: Mary Foy
Mary Foy (1862–1962) was the first woman to be head librarian of the Los Angeles Public Library.

Affectionately known to her students as "Madame," **Tamara Caudill** is an associate professor of French at Jacksonville University. She spends her workdays teaching all levels of language, literature, and culture and devotes her nights, weekends, and summers to the care of her three beautiful children. *Fast Famous Women* is her first foray into creative writing, having previously resigned herself to emails, syllabi, and academic essays on twelfth-century literature—none of which anyone actually reads.

Wrote about: Eleanor of Aquitaine
Eleanor of Aquitaine (1122–1204) served as queen of both France and England in the twelfth century.

*Coauthored with Kathy Krause

Kelly Cecchini is a full-time lecturer in the Harrington School of Communications, Department of Professional and Public Writing, at the University of Rhode Island. She is the former English Department chair at Manchester High School in Manchester, Connecticut. Kelly has also taught as an adjunct in the First-Year Writing program at the University of Connecticut, several Connecticut state community colleges, and Southern New Hampshire University. She allegedly retired in 2021, but we can all see how that turned out. Kelly is now happily living her artsy-seaside-hippie-beach-pad dream in Westerly, Rhode Island.

Wrote about: Mary G. Harris (Mother) Jones
Activist and labor organizer Mother Jones (1837–1930) co-founded the socialist trade union Industrial Workers of the World.

Dr. Gail Choate, activist, author, and adventurer, is a dedicated political scientist. She analyzes and amplifies the voices of "We the People" through her exploration of grassroots activism, electoral politics, and identity. After two distinct but equally successful careers, when the youngest of her four children flew the coop, she sold the family home and embarked on a backpacking adventure through Europe, sparking her research and culminating in her PhD. In her most recent project, Dr. Choate chronicles the hope, courage, and indomitable spirit of grassroots resistance in the contemporary American South.

Wrote about: Fannie Lou Hamer
Fannie Lou Hamer (1917–1977) was a women's rights activist and a leader in the civil rights movement.

Esther Cohen is a nonprofit management professional who started her career as an Off-Broadway stage manager and now directs operations at an international relief and development agency. Her photo can be found in the dictionary next to the phrase "liberal arts major." Esther loves her family, her friends, New Jersey, Paris, and really good bourbon—usually in that order but, hey, some days are better than others. Esther has a BA from Dartmouth College and an MFA from Columbia University.

Wrote about: Diana Rigg
Dame Diana Rigg (1938–2020) was an English actress of stage and screen.

Susan Cossette lives and writes in Minneapolis, Minnesota. Author of *Peggy Sue Messed Up*, she is a recipient of the University of Connecticut's Wallace Stevens Poetry Prize. A two-time Pushcart Prize nominee, look for her work in *Rust and Moth*, *ONE ART*, *As It Ought to Be*, *Anti-Heroin Chic*, the *Amethyst Review*, *Crow & Cross Keys*, *Loch Raven Review*, and the anthologies *Tuesdays at Curley's* and *After the Equinox*. She is director of Annual Giving at a prep school but secretly wishes she was a member of the English department. Be sure to ask about her cats, Sylvia and Chuck.

Wrote about: Marguerite Antonia Radclyffe Hall
Radclyffe Hall (1880–1943) was an English poet and author best known for her groundbreaking work in queer literature.

Kimberly "Kimba" Dalferes is a skilled king salmon slayer and estate sale junkie who sometimes writes funny. Her accomplishments include successfully threading a sewing bobbin, landing a thirty-five-pound Alaskan king salmon, and scoring a ceramic sangria pitcher at an estate sale for $1. A proud Florida State University alumna, she often sings the Seminole fight song out loud for no reason other than she remembers the words. She's a published author whose column "Dock Tale Hour" has been featured in *Laker Magazine* since 2014. She divides her time between Fairfax and Smith Mountain Lake, Virginia. Visit her at www.kimdalferes.com.

Wrote about: Mae West
Mae West (1893–1980) was an actress, singer, comedian, and playwright.

Julie Danis is a writer, storyteller, and former global marketing/advertising executive. She recently wrote and performed her solo show, *Life&#39's Too Short ... and So Am I*, at Chicago's Lifeline Theater's 2024 Fillet of Solo Festival. Other credits include writing for the award-winning documentary film *The Girl Who Wore Freedom*, contributing essays to *Fast Fallen Women* (Woodhall Press, 2023), and *Storyteller's True Stories About Love*, volume 1 (Chicago Writer's Press, 2022). As a business humorist, she wrote a *Chicago Tribune* column called "Living" and contributed commentary to "Marketplace" radio.

Wrote about: Lily Tomlin
Lily Tomlin (b. 1939) is an Emmy and Grammy winner, actor, comedian, writer, singer, and producer.

Carole DeSanti is a writer, editor, and teacher. Her first novel, *The Unruly Passions of Eugénie R.* (2012), was a *New York Times* Editors' Choice selection. Her second, *Plunder*, reimagines the eighteenth-century pirates Anne Bonny and Mary Read. As vice president and executive editor at Viking Penguin for many years, Carole was known for her commitment to women writers and bringing forward marginalized voices and points of view. She has written for the *New York Times*, *The Guardian*, *Women's Review of Books*, and other publications and most recently was Elizabeth Drew Professor of English Language and Literature at Smith College.

Wrote about: Anne Bonny and Mary Read
Anne Bonny and Mary Read were two of the only women pirates in recorded history.

Dimple Dhabalia is a writer, podcaster, facilitator, and coach with more than twenty years of experience working at the intersection of leadership, mindful awareness, and storytelling. In 2021 Dimple founded Roots in the Clouds, a boutique consulting firm specializing in using the power of story to heal organizational trauma and moral injury. Dimple is the best-selling author of *Tell Me My Story—Challenging the Narrative of Service Before Self* and the creator and host of two podcasts, *Service without Sacrifice* and *What Would Ted Lasso Do?* Follow her @dimpstory across all social media platforms and on Substack at "dear humanitarian."

Wrote about: Vijaya Lakshmi Pandit
Indian freedom fighter, diplomat, and politician Vijaya Lakshmi Pandit (1900–1990) served as president of the United Nations General Assembly.

 **Dr. Aynsley Diamond** is associate vice president of academic affairs for the Connecticut State College and University System. She currently holds the rank of practitioner faculty at Johnson & Wales University, where she teaches a curriculum design and development course in the Educational Leadership Doctoral program. The author of the Adaptive Military Transition Theory, Dr. Diamond is a fierce advocate for veteran, active duty, and military-affiliated student populations and seeks to support their transition to higher education via policy action and research.

Wrote about: Billie Jean King
Billie Jean King (b. 1943) is an American former world number-1 tennis player who has won thirty-nine Grand Slam titles.

 **Katherine Duarte** is a graduate of the University of Connecticut. She is a fan of all things fantasy and updates her Goodreads account more than a writer changes words. In her literature classes she'd say that her favorite book is *The Robber Bride* (because she loves talking about moms as much as Tony loves talking about war), when in truth it's probably still *Heartless* by Marissa Meyer or Holly Black's next big release. Her work has been published in *New Square*, *Inverted Syntax*, and writer and professor Gina Barreca's book of essays, *Fast Fallen Women: 75 Essays of Flash Nonfiction*.

Wrote about: Sandra Cisneros
Sandra Cisneros (b. 1954) is an award-winning poet, novelist, essayist, and artist.

 **Niamh Emerson** immigrated to the United States from Ireland with her parents and younger sister, but not before climbing Knocknarea (Queen Maeve's grave) at least twice. A proud graduate of the University of Connecticut and Yale University, Niamh really showed her mom what you can do with an English degree (get another one, of course!). Niamh is the editor of *Your Yale*, a weekly newsletter for Yale staff. She and her husband, Paul, are raising three wonderful children: big sister Matilda and twins Patrick and Jack. Yes, she has her hands full. No, she doesn't really know how she does it.

Wrote about: Queen Maeve of Ireland
Queen Maeve of Ireland is a figure of Irish folklore who was said to be a warrior of great strength.

 **Bonnie Jean Feldkamp** is the opinion editor for Pulitzer Prize–winning *Louisville Courier Journal*. She is also an award-winning syndicated columnist with Creators Syndicate. Her TEDx Talk explains "Contempt Versus Connections in Online Communication."

Wrote about: Erma Bombeck
Erma Bombeck (1927–1996) was a syndicated columnist and humorist.

Sophia Gabriel is a passionate storyteller from Fairfield, Connecticut. Having a love for writing from a young age, her mother, Kathy, encouraged her to pursue a BA in English and American studies at the University of Connecticut (sometimes Mother does know best). Sophia found joy in bringing her passion for writing to the corporate world through marketing and has worked with brands in the fashion and beauty industries since graduating in 2021. A proud Auntie, her favorite place to be is with her niece and nephew, coffee in one hand, pen in the other, crafting prose that stirs the soul.

Wrote about: Ruth Bader Ginsberg
Lawyer and jurist Ruth Bader Ginsberg (1933–2020) served as an associate justice of the Supreme Court of the United States.

Darien Hsu Gee lives and writes from the island of Hawaiʻi. An award-winning essayist and nonfiction author, her work has appeared in the *Tampa Review, River Styx, CALYX, Tupelo Quarterly,* and *Poetry Northwest,* among others. Her novels have been published in eleven countries. She is a Poetry Society of America Chapbook fellow and Sustainable Arts Foundation grant recipient. Darien recently served as the Mark Twain Distinguished Writer-in-Residence for the Creative Writing Program at the University of Connecticut.

Wrote about: Joyce Chen
Joyce Chen (1917–1994) was a chef, restauranteur, author, and entrepreneur.

Kelley Gifford is a recent graduate of the University of Connecticut, where she studied English. While at UConn, she interned at the Connecticut Writing Project and was a poetry panelist and interviews editor at the literary journal the *Long River Review*. She currently works at her local library and hopes to continue her studies in the field of library science. In her free time, Kelley is a show skier, performing gravity-defying tricks on water skis, and an award-winning knitter known for her colorful designs.

Wrote about: Georgia O'Keeffe
Georgia O'Keeffe (1887–1986) was a renowned modernist painter.

Elena (Laney) Greenberg is a divorce lawyer in New York. Notwithstanding, and to counterbalance the rigors of her practice, she has actively pursued her interests and maintained her enthusiasm for film, music, and literature throughout her career.

Wrote about: Elizabeth Taylor
Actress Dame Elizabeth Taylor (1932–2011) was one of the most popular stars of classical Hollywood cinema.

 **Kim A. Hanson** is an award-winning, accredited business communicator, retired from corporate consulting and happily rediscovering her freelance writing roots. Kim received her BS in English literature/writing from Fairfield University and has written for the *New York Times, Connecticut Magazine,* and the *Examiner* website, as well as a number of industry magazines. Prior to her consulting work, she held communication directorships within various US and global corporations, one of which was the parent company of Universal Studios. Kim and her husband have one adult son, Zack, and numerous Italian American and Hanson relatives.

Wrote about: Margaret Sanger
Margaret Sanger (1879–1966) was a birth control activist, sex educator, writer, and nurse.

 **Emily Heiden's** writing has been published in the *Washington Post, Electric Lit, Lit Hub,* the *Seattle Times,* the *Hartford Courant, Brevity Magazine, Colorado Review,* and elsewhere. Her essay "Uncharted" appeared in *Fast Fallen Women* (2023), and her essay "Why I Gave Up Dating Online" appeared in *Fast Funny Women* (2021). Her essay "Scenes from July 2013" was published in *Don't Look Now: Things We Wish We Hadn't Seen* by Mad Creek Books (2020). She holds a PhD in literature and creative writing from the University of Cincinnati and an MFA in creative nonfiction from George Mason University.

Wrote about: Simone de Beauvoir
Simone de Beauvoir (1908–1986) was a French existentialist philosopher and feminist activist.

Karen S. Henry collaborated with director Herbert Blau and Kraken in creating and performing *Elsinore*, based on *Hamlet*, and *Crooked Eclipses*, based on Shakespeare's sonnets. She co-founded the Boston Theater Group, producing works based on Kafka, Ovid, Shakespeare, and contemporary poetry. With composer W. Newell Hendricks, Karen received NEA grants for the operas *The Cell* and *Ascona*. She currently performs with Row Twelve Contemporary Music Ensemble. Her poems have appeared in *BoomerLitMag, Cathexis Northwest, Crosswinds, Night Forest, NonBinary, Pine Row, Stoneboat, Zoetic Press's Literary Whip* podcast, and elsewhere. Her chapbook, *All Will Fall Away*, was published by Finishing Line Press.

Wrote about: Martha Graham
Martha Graham (1894–1991) was a modern dancer, choreographer, and teacher whose style and technique reshaped American dance.

Polly Ingraham has had a career in high schools, both as an English teacher and a school-to-career counselor. Completing Grub Street's Memoir Incubator program in 2018, she continued working on a book manuscript about her life as an unconventional clergy spouse, currently seeking publication. She has attended workshops at the Madeline Island School of the Arts, the New York State Writers Institute, Wesleyan University Writers Conference, and the Iowa Writers Festival. Her work has appeared in the *Boston Globe Sunday Magazine, Tikkun, Dartmouth Alumni Magazine*, and on National Public Radio. Last fall, an excerpt of her memoir was nominated by Unleash Press for a Pushcart Prize. Her blog is pastorswifeblog.com.

Wrote about: Mary Ingraham Bunting Smith
Former president of Radcliffe College Mary Ingraham Bunting (1910–1998) was an influential scientist in the field of bacterial genetics.

Pascale Joachim is a young writer with aspirations of sustaining herself by giving her ideas the attention they deserve. Her main priority now is freeing herself from student debt, but she keeps the dream alive by writing for her local paper and participating in her community writing group. Feel free to connect with her via email at pjoachim255@gmail.com or Instagram @pascaleejoachim.

Wrote about: Toni Morrison
Toni Morrison (1931–2019) was a Nobel- and Pulitzer Prize–winning novelist, editor, and professor.

Krisela Karaja is an Albanian American writer. A former US Fulbright Student Research Fellow to Albania, her interests include contemporary poetry in the post-communist, democratic transition and comparative literature in English, Albanian, Spanish, and Danish. Krisela holds a master of fine arts from UMass Boston. Her work can be found in *Fast Funny Women*, *Container*, and *Write on the Dot*.

Wrote about: Jane Smiley
Jane Smiley (b. 1949) is a Pulitzer Prize–winning novelist.

Pamela Katz is a screenwriter and author most known for her films with legendary director Margarethe von Trotta, including *Rosenstrasse* and *Hannah Arendt* (a *New York Times* critic A. O. Scott's "Top Ten Film"), as well as her book, *The Partnership: Brecht, Weill, Three Women and Germany on the Brink* published by Doubleday/Nan A. Talese. She is currently working on a screenplay about Simone Weil's participation in the Spanish Civil War. Pamela has published essays in many collections and written for the *New York Times*, *Salmagundi*, *Differences*, and *Aufbau*, but she is especially honored to be among Barreca's spectacular community of funny, fierce, fallen, and now famous women. Pamela teaches screenwriting at the NYU Graduate School of Film.

Wrote about: Margarethe von Trotta
Margarethe von Trotta (b. 1942) is a German film director, screenwriter, and actress.

Betsy Golden Kellem is a scholar of the unusual. Her writing has appeared in venues including *The Atlantic*, *Vanity Fair*, the *Washington Post*, the *Public Domain Review*, *Smithsonian*, *Atlas Obscura*, *Bandwagon*, and *Slate*. Betsy serves on the boards of the Barnum Museum and the Circus Historical Society and is a regional Emmy winner for her *Showman's Shorts* series on P. T. Barnum. You can follow her work at drinkswithdeadpeople.com. If you ask nicely, she will juggle knives for you.

Wrote about: Annie Oakley
Annie Oakley (1860–1926) was a champion sharpshooter and Western folk hero.

Nyanka Kizzy writes for pleasure and writes what her younger self would've loved to read. When she's not enjoying her time with her family, she can be found voraciously consuming books or television shows. Her work has been featured in the *Caribbean Writer*, the *Ponder Review*, and several other publications. You can find her weekly newsletter, *Consume, The Blog*, on Substack, where she writes personal essays, fiction, pop culture critique, and poetry. She hopes her writing makes Black women and girls feel seen.

Wrote about: Audre Lorde
Audre Lorde (1934–1992) was a noted prose writer, professor, feminist, and civil rights activist.

Cleverly disguised as an English professor at the University of Colorado, Boulder, **Mary Klages** secretly divides her time between searching for new Helen Keller jokes and playing with her Tinkertoys.

Wrote about: Hellen Keller
Co-founder of the ACLU, Helen Keller (1880–1968) was an author, political activist, and disability rights advocate.

Angie Klink has authored twelve books. She has written for the American Writers Museum, *Ms. Magazine, Traces of Indiana History* magazine, and for documentaries narrated by actor Peter Coyote. She holds sixty-two American Advertising Federation ADDY Awards and an honorable mention in the Erma Bombeck Writing Competition. Klink writes about author Evaleen Stein and procured a 2024 Indiana Historical Bureau marker honoring Stein. A recipient of the Excellence in Historic Preservation Medal from the National Society of the Daughters of the American Revolution (their most prestigious award, honoring dedication to preservation, including writing books), Klink holds a BA in communication from Purdue University. For more, visit angieklink.com.

Wrote about: Amelia Earheart
Aviator and writer Amelia Earhart (1897–1939) was the first woman to fly solo across the Atlantic Ocean.

Kathy Krause is emerita professor of French and Medieval Studies at the University of Missouri–Kansas City. Her research focuses on female patronage and female lordship in northern France and Flanders in the long thirteenth-century, which is relevant to her coauthored piece in this anthology, as one of the female patrons she works on was almost Eleanor of Aquitaine's granddaughter-in-law. But that is a story for another volume! When not holed up in manuscript reading rooms, she enjoys hiking, knitting, and encouraging her younger colleagues.

Wrote about: Eleanor of Aquitaine
Eleanor of Aquitaine (1122–1204) served as queen of both France and England in the twelfth century. *Coauthored with Tamara Caudill

 **Mary Elaine Lasley** is a writer, artist, and graduate of UConn's English program. When not writing or drawing, she spends much of her time pouring coffee, wandering the graveyard, watching movies, and making absurd proclamations. If you ask, she will let you take a shot out of the Lord Byron souvenir glass.

Wrote about: Mary Shelley
Mary Shelley (1797–1851) was a novelist, short story writer, and essayist best known for writing *Frankenstein*.

 **Caroline Leavitt** is the *New York Times* best-selling author of thirteen novels, most recently *Days of Wonder*, a most anticipated read from Read with Jenna Page, Oprah Daily, Zibby Owens, and more. She is the recipient of fellowships from the New York Foundation of the Arts and from the Mid Atlantic Arts/New Jersey Individual Artist foundation, as well as being a finalist for the Sundance Screenwriters Lab. Her work has appeared in the *New York Times* "Modern Love" column, *New York Magazine*, the *Daily Beast*, and more. A book critic for *People* and for AARP's *The Ethel*, she is the co-founder of the book promotion platform, A Mighty Blaze.

Wrote about: Fanny Brice
Fanny Brice (1891–1951) was an influential comedian, singer, and theater and film actress.

Phillis Levin's sixth collection, *An Anthology of Rain*, is forthcoming from Barrow Street Press in April 2025. Her previous collection, *Mr. Memory & Other Poems* (Penguin Books, 2016), was a finalist for the *Los Angeles Times* Book Prize. Levin's honors include the Poetry Society of America's Norma Farber First Book Award, a Fulbright Scholar Award to Slovenia, the Amy Lowell Poetry Travelling Scholarship, a Guggenheim Fellowship, and a National Endowment for the Arts grant. Widely anthologized, her work has appeared in *The Atlantic, Kenyon Review*, the *New Republic*, the *New Yorker, Paris Review, Plume, Poetry*, and the *Yale Review*.

Wrote about: Molly Peacock
Molly Peacock (b. 1947) is an essayist, short fiction writer, and biographer.

Leighann Lord is a veteran stand-up comedian and author. She's been seen on Comedy Central, HBO, and Showtime's *Funny Women of a Certain Age*. She has written several humor books, including *Dict Jokes: Alternate Definitions for Words You've Probably Never Heard of But Will Definitely Never Forget, Real Women Do It Standing Up: Stories from the Career of a Very Funny Lady*, and *People with Parents: The Podcast Transcripts*. Leighann earned her BA in journalism and creative writing from Baruch College, City University of New York, and she is a firm supporter of the Oxford comma.

Wrote about: Maya Angelou
Maya Angelou (1928–2014) was an acclaimed poet, memoirist, and civil rights activist.

The Hon. Rev. Dr. Adrienne R. Lotson, Esq., is guided by a quest for the passionate life. This quest has taken her through careers as a pioneering sports attorney, spiritual retreat leader, administrative law judge, cultural anthropologist, and artist. Adrienne has engaged with audiences throughout the United States, Europe, Israel, Africa, and the Caribbean, including as a featured storyteller with *The Moth*. The first Black woman president in the 112-year history of Dartmouth College's alumni association, Dr. Lotson ran her first marathon at 50, earned a PhD at 55, and has her eyes set on new adventures in media and publishing.

Wrote about: Katherine Dunham
Dancer and choreographer Katherine Dunham (1909–2006) was a pioneer in dance anthropology.

Angela C. McConney is an attorney and has served in public service for more than two decades. A longtime leader in the Massachusetts Bar, she just concluded a two-year term as president of the Massachusetts Bar Foundation, the first president of color in the organization's fifty-eight-year history. McConney was honored by *Massachusetts Lawyers Weekly* with the 2012 Award for Excellence in Diversity and the 2016 Top Women in the Law Award. She received the Massachusetts Black Women Attorneys 2021 Public Interest Award. McConney lives in Milton, Massachusetts.

Wrote about: Barbara Jordan
Barbara Jordan (1936–1996) was the first Black woman from the South to be elected to the United States Congress.

 **Grace McFadden** is a radio reporter and amateur poet from Connecticut. She majored in English and American studies at the University of Connecticut. She has worked at several radio stations running errands, writing stories, and replying to angry listeners. She spent four years as a DJ at UConn's college and community radio station, WHUS, before moving on to other endeavors. She currently resides in Rochester, New York.

Wrote about: Alison Steele
Alison Steele (1937–1995) was a writer, producer, correspondent, and radio personality.

 **Lara Scalzi Meek** is a proud Nutmegger, born and raised in Connecticut. She is a graduate of the University of Connecticut, with a BA in English, a minor in women's studies, and a creative writing concentration. Lara currently lives in Oakland, California, with her husband, where she is a Bay Area performer, mother, and writer of fiction during preschool hours. She enjoys historic dive bars, coffee, reading, and costume opportunities.

Wrote about: Tammy Duckworth
Politician Tammy Duckworth (b. 1968) currently serves as the United States Senator from Illinois.

 **Sydney Melocowsky** is a recent graduate of the University of Connecticut and is currently pursuing her MA in creative writing at Bath Spa University. She uses language and the art of breaking formal tradition to express her experience as a neurodivergent writer and focuses on producing work that encourages literary empathy as an alternative to accessibility. Her dedication to inclusion through narrative is the catalyst of her academic career, as she hopes to complete a manuscript that bridges the credibility associated with academic research and the compressed power of previously structureless voices.

Wrote about: Gertrude Stein
Gertrude Stein (1874–1946) was a feminist novelist, poet, and collector of avant-garde art.

 **Maggie Mitchell** is the author of the novel *Pretty Is*, which the *New York Times* called "a stunning, multi-layered debut." Her short fiction has appeared in the *South Carolina Review, New Ohio Review, American Literary Review, Green Mountains Review*, and elsewhere. She has been awarded fellowships at the Sewanee Writers' Conference, the Vermont Studio Center, and the Millay Colony for the Arts. She lives in Atlanta.

Wrote about: Virginia Woolf
Novelist Virgina Woolf (1882–1941) was considered one of the most influential modernist twentieth-century authors.

 **Rory Monaco** says, "My friends joke that it's hard to catch me between four walls, but they're right. Even when writing or reading, I'm most likely barefoot outside. Whether I'm sticking my feet in the ocean or lying in the grass on sunny days, the words I write will forever be inspired by the world around me."

Wrote about: Mary Oliver
Mary Oliver (1935–2019) was a Pulitzer Prize– and National Book Award–winning poet.

 **Margaret Anne Mary Moore** is the author of the bestselling memoir *Bold, Brave, and Breathless: Reveling in Childhood's Splendiferous Glories While Facing Disability and Loss*. She earned an MFA in creative nonfiction and poetry from Fairfield University. Margaret is an editor and the marketing coordinator at Woodhall Press and an ambassador for PRC-Saltillo. Her writing appears or is forthcoming in *Kairos: A Journal of Rhetoric, Technology, Pedagogy, America Magazine*, and *Brevity's Nonfiction Blog*, among other publications. Connect with her at margaretannemarymoore.com.

Wrote about: Bethany Hamilton
Bethany Hamilton (b. 1990) is a professional surfer and writer who survived a shark attack.

Brenda Murphy lives in Maryland. She is the author of more than twenty books, mostly about American drama and theater. Recently she has been concentrating on historical fiction. Her latest books include *When Light Breaks Through: A Salem Witch Trials Story* (2023), which focuses on the effort to bring peace to Salem after the trials; *Becoming Carlotta: A Biographical Novel* (2018), based on the life of the notorious actress Carlotta Monterey; and *After the Voyage: An Irish American Story* (2016), based on the experience of her immigrant family at the turn of the twentieth century.

Wrote about: Jane Fonda
Jane Fonda (b. 1937) is an Academy Award–winning actress and activist.

Ebony Murphy joined the English faculty of Saint Ann's School in Brooklyn in 2022. Ebony, a University of Connecticut alumna, has trained with Emerge California, Los Angeles African American Women's Public Policy Institute, and ADL LA's Michael LaPrade Holocaust Education Institute and was selected for the Facing History's California Civic Fellows Program. In 2018 she was a fellow of the Religious Literacy Summer Institute for Educators at Harvard Divinity School. She serves on the board of the Feminist Press, which publishes writing by people who share an activist spirit and a belief in choice and equality.

Wrote about: Flo Kennedy
Lawyer Florynce Kennedy (1916–2000) was a radical feminist, civil rights activist, and lecturer.

Elizabeth Norton is a writer and singer. A graduate of Sarah Lawrence College, she worked for many years as a science writer for MCI Communications, the Charles A. Dana Foundation, and *Science Magazine*. Drawing on her experience with singing, breath work, stage fright, and neurobiology, she coauthored *The End of Stress as We Know It*, a book about the science of stress. She is currently working on a novel and taking an online computer course—yes, she is Learning to Code. Born in Brooklyn, New York, she lives in Connecticut on a small farm encroached upon by invasive plant species.

Wrote about: Janet Yellen
Janet Yellen (b. 1946) currently serves as the seventy-eighth US secretary of the treasury.

Maria Parenteau graduated from the University of Connecticut in 2020 with a degree in English and concentrations in both sociology and creative writing, as well as having received her Paralegal Certification from Boston University in 2021. Maria currently works as a paralegal and plans to attend law school beginning in the fall of 2024. In addition to pursuing a career in law, Maria enjoys both reading and writing and has been published several times. She also enjoys spending time with family and friends, playing soccer and basketball, and trips to the beach with her dog, Bruno.

Wrote about: Malala Yousafzai
Female education activist Malala Yousafzai (b. 1997) is the world's youngest Nobel Peace Prize laureate.

 **Emily Parrow** holds a BS and MA in history from Liberty University and works at The Preservation Society of Newport County. She served on the selection committee for the 2024 Edith Wharton–Straw Dog Writers Guild Writers-in-Residence program and is a contributor to the New England Historical Society, a popular blog. Emily is currently coauthoring an essay on President Chester Arthur's visits to Newport, Rhode Island, in the 1880s. Her favorite Edith Wharton novel is *The Custom of the Country*.

Wrote about: Edith Wharton
Writer and designer Edith Wharton (1862–1937) was the first woman to win the Pulitzer Prize in Fiction.

 **Molly Peacock** is the author of eight books of poetry, including *The Widow's Crayon Box* and *Cornucopia: New & Selected Poems*, as well as *A Friend Sails in on a Poem*, about her friendship with Phillis Levin. She is also the author of two biographies: *The Paper Garden: Mrs. Delany Begins Her Life's Work at 72* and *Flower Diary: Mary Hiester Reid Paints, Travels, Marries & Opens a Door*. Peacock co-founded Poetry in Motion on New York's subways and buses, founded the Best Canadian Poetry series, and, most recently, created the Secret Poetry Room at Binghamton University.

Wrote about: Phillis Levin
Phillis Levin (b. 1954) is a poet, essayist, and editor.

Trace Peterson is a poet, editor, and literary scholar. Her book *Since I Moved In* was reissued by Chax Press in a new edition, with an introduction by Joy Ladin in 2019. She is the co-editor of *Arrive on Wave: Collected Poems of Gil Ott* (Chax, 2016) and of the groundbreaking anthology *Troubling the Line: Trans and Genderqueer Poetry and Poetics* (Nightboat Books, 2013). Peterson also edits *EOAGH*, a small press and literary journal that has won two Lambda Literary Awards and a National Jewish Book Award. She is currently a visiting assistant professor at UConn–Storrs.

Wrote about: Joy Landin

Joy Ladin (b. 1961) is a poet, literary scholar, nationally recognized speaker, and the first openly transgender professor at an Orthodox Jewish institution.

An educator since 1995, **Rachel Sutz Pienta** has worked with students from preschool to the postgraduate level. She taught women's studies courses for a decade, with an emphasis on fast famous, and furious women. Rachel's writing has been published in anthologies including *The 21st Century Motherhood Movement*, *The New Politics of the Textbook*, and *Voices in Medical Sociology*. She currently serves on the editorial board for the *Journal of Extension* and the *Journal of Online Learning Research and Practice*. She lives on the northern Florida Gulf Coast with her husband, David, and a Russian Blue rescue cat named Luna.

Wrote about: Zora Neale Hurston

Writer and anthropologist Zora Neale Hurston (1891–1960) was considered one of the preeminent writers of twentieth-century African American literature.

Cheryl Della Pietra is author of the novel *Gonzo Girl*, inspired by her time as Hunter S. Thompson's assistant in the early '90s. She has written for many national magazines, such as *Marie Claire* and *Redbook*, and has participated in several spoken-word performances, including the MOTH Mainstage in San Francisco. She lives in Branford, Connecticut, with her husband and son.

Wrote about: Alex Guarnaschelli
Alex Guarnaschelli (b. 1969) is a chef, cookbook author, and television personality.

Mimi Pond has been a cartoonist and writer for over thirty years, producing five humor books in the 1980s, including *The Valley Girls' Guide to Life*. She wrote the first episode of *The Simpsons*, "Simpsons Roasting on an Open Fire." Her 2014 graphic novel, *Over Easy*, published by Drawn & Quarterly, was on the *New York Times* Best Seller List and won a PEN Award. The second volume of this story, *The Customer Is Always Wrong*, was published in 2017. Her current project is a work of non-fiction about Britain's storied Mitford Sisters, to be published in 2025 by Drawn & Quarterly.

Wrote about: Jessica Mitford
Jessica Mitford (1917–1996) was a writer and muckraking journalist.

Pam Quinn is a law professor at Drexel University, where she teaches international law, family law, and a seminar on the US Supreme Court. She lives in Philadelphia with her fiancé, almost-grown children, dogs, and a cat.

Wrote about: Susan B. Anthony

Susan B. Anthony (1820–1906) was a social reformer who played a pivotal role in the women's suffrage movement.

Lara Dotson-Renta is an educator and writer based outside Chicago. She holds a PhD in Romance languages from UPenn, with a focus on Spanish and French postcolonial literatures and a sub-specialization in African studies. She also has an MA from NYU (Paris) and a BA from Dartmouth College. Her academic book *Immigration, Popular Culture, and the Re-Routing of European Muslim Identity* was published by Palgrave Macmillan in 2012. She has published articles in popular media outlets including the *New York Times*, *Washington Post*, and *The Atlantic* on topics ranging from education to parenting. She is also a 500-hour RYT yogi.

Wrote about: Sonia Sotomayor
Lawyer and jurist Sonia Sotomayor (b. 1954) currently serves as an associate justice of the Supreme Court of the United States.

 **Heidi Rockefeller** lives in Connecticut with her husband of twenty-eight years and her two adult daughters living nearby. Most days you can find Heidi with a bit of knitting or, when it is warm out, puttering in her garden. After a failed attempt at retirement a couple of years ago, Heidi is back at work tidying the worlds of her favorite clients. Her main goal these days is maintaining a close-knit family and making the world a better place by helping people as she goes.

Wrote about: Maria Montessori
Maria Montessori (1870–1952) was an Italian physician and educator.

 **Laura Rockefeller** has been told she's related to "The Rockefellers" but hasn't gotten a penny out of it. Nonetheless, she is one of the richest Rockefellers you'll ever know. She is rich in family, living in Connecticut with her loving husband, Eli, and spunky tortie, Sequoia. When Laura isn't home watching Soft White Underbelly interviews, you will likely find her roaming Connecticut exploring restaurants, museums, and parks to feature on her CT-centric Instagram page, @thenomadicnutmegger.

Wrote about: Temple Grandin
Temple Grandin (b. 1947) is a prominent author and speaker on autism and animal behavior.

Laura Rossi-Totten is an author, podcast producer, and public relations expert who ran publicity campaigns for bestselling authors at New York City's top publishers, including Random House, The Dial Press, Viking Penguin, and W. W. Norton, before founding Laura Rossi Public Relations. Appearing in the *New York Times*, *Psychology Today*, the *Huffington Post*, and on NPR, Laura majored in English and communications at the University of Connecticut. She volunteers for A Mighty Blaze and local NPR and hopes that she and her daughter, Julia, will publish essays together. Connect with her at laurarossipublicrelations.com.

Wrote about: Taylor Swift
Taylor Swift (b. 1989) is a Grammy award–winning singer-songwriter who has vastly influenced the music industry.
*Coauthored with her daughter, Julia Totten

Amy Hartl Sherman has done improvisational and stand-up comedy, was a flight attendant, is a wife and mother, loves animals, and writes accordingly. Find her on Facebook or follow her on TikTok: @amysherman1funnybroad.

Wrote about: Marilyn Monroe
Actress and singer Marilyn Monroe (1926–1962) was an emblem of the sexual revolution of the 1950s and 1960s.

Jane Smiley just keeps writing stuff. Oh, okay: Jane Smiley is the author of many novels and works of nonfiction. Her latest novel is *Lucky*.

Wrote about: Jane Lynch
Jane Lynch (b. 1960) is an Emmy award–winning actress and comedian.

Sarah Strauss is professor of anthropology and climate adaptation at Worcester Polytechnic Institute (WPI) in Massachusetts. She taught at the University of Wyoming for twenty-four years and has been visiting faculty at Uni Fribourg in Switzerland and Pondicherry University in India. Her books include *Positioning Yoga* (2005), *Weather, Climate, Culture* (2004, edited with Ben Orlove), and *Cultures of Energy* (2013, edited by Stephanie Rupp and Thomas Love). As a big fan of both Margaret Mead and Gina Barreca, she has had a blast working on this book!

Wrote about: Margaret Mead
Margaret Mead (1901–1978) was a cultural anthropologist, author, and speaker on women's rights.

Julia Totten is a Pre-Med student at the University of Virginia, double majoring in biochemistry and music. Julia is a UVA Miller Arts Scholar with a flute performance concentration and is a Dean's List Distinguished Student. She loves to travel, cook, listen to music, and spend time with family and friends. Julia lives in Rhode Island. *Fast Famous Women* marks Julia's author debut.

Wrote about: Taylor Swift
Taylor Swift (b. 1989) is a Grammy award–winning singer-songwriter who has vastly influenced the music industry.
*Coauthored with her mother, Laura Rossi-Totten.

Alison Umminger is the author of the critically acclaimed novel *American Girls* as well as a certified spiritual director and retreat leader. When she's not busy with her own Ramona, she loves leading contemplative retreats and teaching creative writing.

Wrote about: Beverly Cleary
Beverly Cleary (1916–2021) was a writer of children's and young adult fiction.

Beth Welch is a lifelong reader, especially of Louisa May Alcott, and longtime editor of history books for college students. She sits on the Board of the Newburyport Literary Association and teaches classes in her local continuing-education program, most recently on Fast Famous/Funny/ Fierce Woman Nora Ephron. Beth lives in Newbury, Massachusetts, a short drive from the Alcotts' Orchard House, with her husband and cat.

Wrote about: Louisa May Alcott
Louisa May Alcott (1832–1888) was a novelist, short story writer, and poet best known for writing *Little Women*.

Contributor Information

Kelley Cecchini

Gorn, Elliot J. *Mother Jones: The Most Dangerous Woman in America.* Hill and Wang, New York, 2001.

Jones, Mary Harris. *Autobiography of Mother Jones.* Charles Kerr and Co., Chicago. 1925. Unabridged reprint, Dover Publications, Inc. Mineola, New York. 2004.

"Meet Mother Jones." Almanac.Com, 16 Feb. 2024, www.almanac.com/meet-mother-jones. Mother Jones.

BIOGRAPHY. https://www.biography.com/activists/mother-jones

Gail Choate

Hamer, Fannie Lou. 1967. *To Praise Our Bridges: An Autobiography of Mrs. Fannie Lou Hamer.* KIPCO.

The American Yawp Reader. "Fannie Lou Hamer: Testimony at the Democratic National Convention 1964" Stanford University Press. https://www.americanyawp.com/reader/27-the-sixties/fannie-lou-hamer-testimony-at-the-democratic-national-convention-1964/

Brooks, Maegan Parker, and Davis W. Houck, eds. "'Until I Am Free, You Are Not Free Either,': Speech Delivered at the University of Wisconsin, Madison, Wisconsin, January 1971." In *The Speeches of Fannie Lou Hamer: To Tell It Like It Is*, 121–30. University Press of Mississippi, 2011. http://www.jstor.org/stable/j.ctt12f641.18.\

Carole DeSanti
"Anne Bonny and Mary Read" by Carole DeSanti
(Copyright symbol) 2024 by Carole DeSanti
Used by permission of Robin Straus Agency, Inc.

Karen Henry
DeMille, Agnes. *Martha: The Life and Work of Martha Graham.*
Random House, 1956.
Graham, Martha. *Blood Memory.* Doubleday, 1991.

Polly Ingraham
Yaffe, Elaine. *Mary Ingraham Bunting: Her Two Lives.* Savannah:
Frederic C. Bell, 2005.

Mary Klages
Joseph P. Lash, *Helen and Teacher: The Story of Helen Keller and Anne Sullivan Macy.* Dell Publishing Company, 1980.
"HK and the Problem of Inspiration Porn" NYT 10/21/2021 by M. Leona Godin

Angie Klink:
John Norberg, *Wings of their Dreams*, (West Lafayette, IN: Purdue University Press, 2007), 174.
George Palmer Putnam, *Soaring Wings: A Biography of Amelia Earhart*, (London, W.C.: George G. Harrap & Co, 1940), 221.
John Norberg, *Ever True: 150 Years of Giant Leaps at Purdue University*, ((West Lafayette, IN: Purdue University Press, 2019), 174.
Amelia Earhart Timeline, Purdue University Archives and Special Collections.
Edward C. Elliott telegram to George Palmer Putnam, March 25, 1937, "Amelia Earhart at Purdue," Purdue Archives and Special Collections, https://earchives.lib.purdue.edu/digital/collection/epurdue/id/198/rec/34.

Angie Klink, *The Deans' Bible: Five Purdue Women and Their Quest for Equality*, (West Lafayette, IN: Purdue University, 2014), 89.

Phillis Levin & Molly Peacock
This essay is drawn from *A Friend Sails in on a Poem* by Molly Peacock, with an "Afterword" by Phillis Levin, from Palimpsest Press, 2022. The quote by Charles Tomlinson is from "The Poem as Initiation," an address at Colgate University, October 30, 1967.

Caroline Leavitt
Caroline Leavitt's new motto is now "Live your life like Fanny Brice."

Margaret Moore
Tom Price, "2008: Teen surfer ministers to others after losing arm in shark attack," *Calvary Chapel Magazine*,
April 30, 2023, https://calvarychapelmagazine.org/articles/bethany-hamilton.
"Bethany Hamilton Biography–Childhood, Life Achievements: Timeline," TheFamousPeople, accessed
Ashtyn Douglas-Rosa, "More Than a Survivor: The Bethany Hamilton Profile," SURFER, July 9, 2018. https://www.surfer.com/features/more-than-a-survivor-the-bethany-hamilton-profile.
Dalton Bartlett, "TWISH: Surfer Bethany Hamilton defies all odds after losing her arm in a shark attack," The Maine Campus, October 31, 2022, https://mainecampus.com/category/sports/2022/10/twish-surfer-bethany-hamilton-defies-all-odds-after-losing-her-arm-in-a-shark-attack.

Trace Peterson
"Performances were not..." from *Personal Interview with Joy Landin*
"Imagine what..." from *Girl in a Bottle* by Joy Landin
"She thinks how 'futile'..." from *Personal Interview with Joy Landin*

Contributor Information

"*Anna Ascher...*" *from* Personal Interview with Joy landin
"a Czech-German Jewish poet..." from *Anna and Me*, afterword to *The Book of Anna* by Joy Landin EOAGH Books, 2021.
"at the top..." from *Girl in a Bottle* by Joy Landin
"Words that weren't mine..." from *Girl in a Bottle* by Joy Landin
" 'someone else', someone who..." from *Girl in a Bottle* by Joy Landin
"For the first time..." from *Girl in a Bottle* by Joy Landin
"My muse is Rage..." from *The Book of Anna by Joy Landin*
"My muse...the muse inspiring..." from *Girl in a Bottle* by Joy Landin
"Inhabit a form..." from *Personal Interview with Joy Landin*

Acknowledgments

It is a pleasure to acknowledge the best of best company and thank David LeGere, Christopher Madden, Margaret Moore, and the whole team at Woodhall Press for making the *Fast Women* series gloriously fun.

Famous was inspired by the amazing Darien Hsu Gee (who writes about Joyce Chen for this collection) because Darien was the one who suggested that asking great women to write about their own inspirations would be the way to go—and so it was!

Mary Lasley designed the spectacular cover art (you can read her essay on Mary Shelley).

Pascale Joachim was an exceptionally astute editor and reader for the manuscript (which includes her essay on Toni Morrison).

Alexander Grant, who worked on the book from the day we decided it would be a book, was essential to every moment of the process and every page of this publication. Alex read, advised, edited, researched, and managed crisis control.

Amelia Sherman worked diligently on *Famous* for this past year, and she was reliably terrific.

Finally, I would like to acknowledge that my husband, Michael Meyer, has always been in favor of Fast Women.